Simple Coloring Book of Letters, Numbers & Shapes For Pre-K

Copyright © 2023 Trina L Conner
All rights reserved
ISBN:9798374610086
Independently published

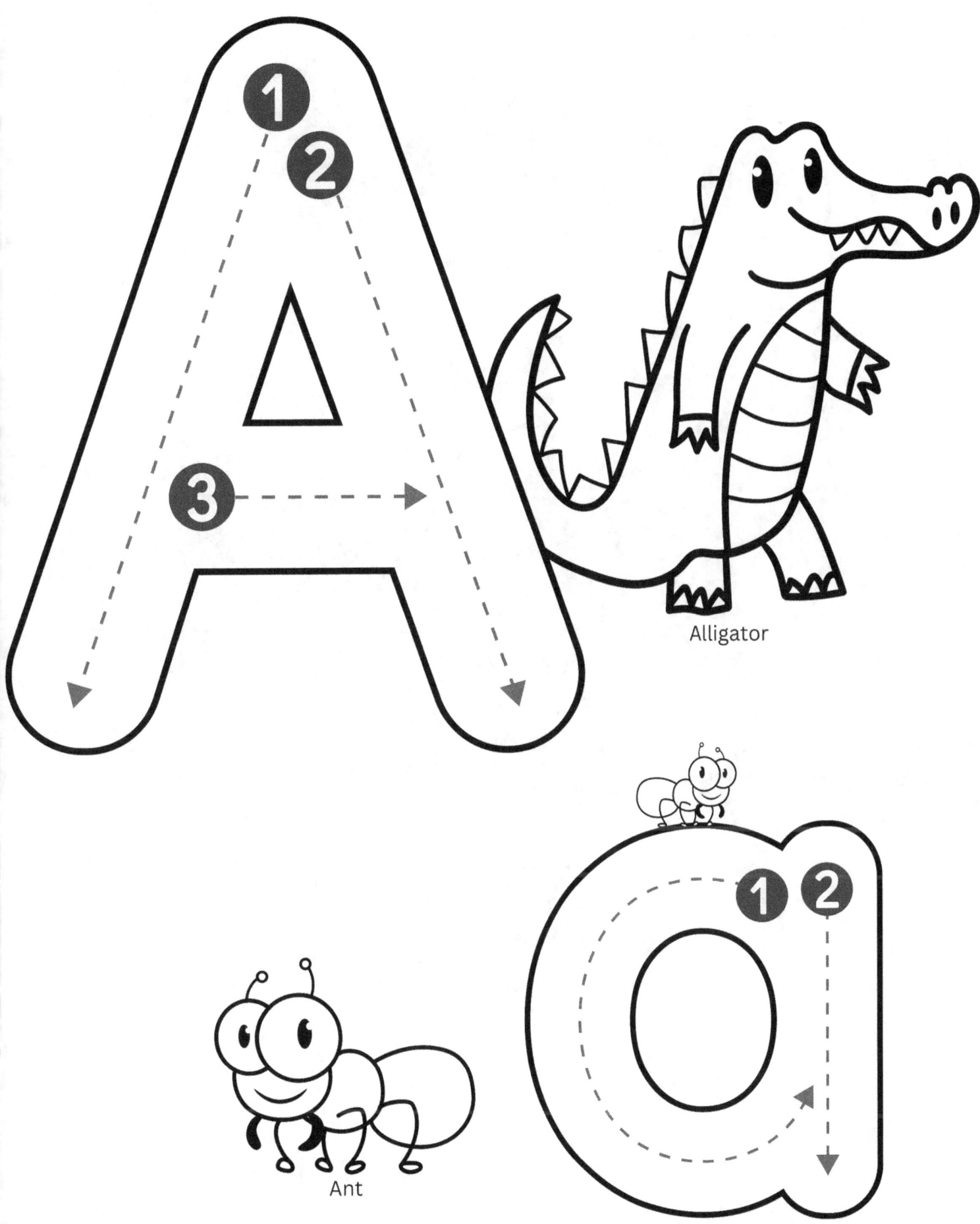
Alligator

Ant

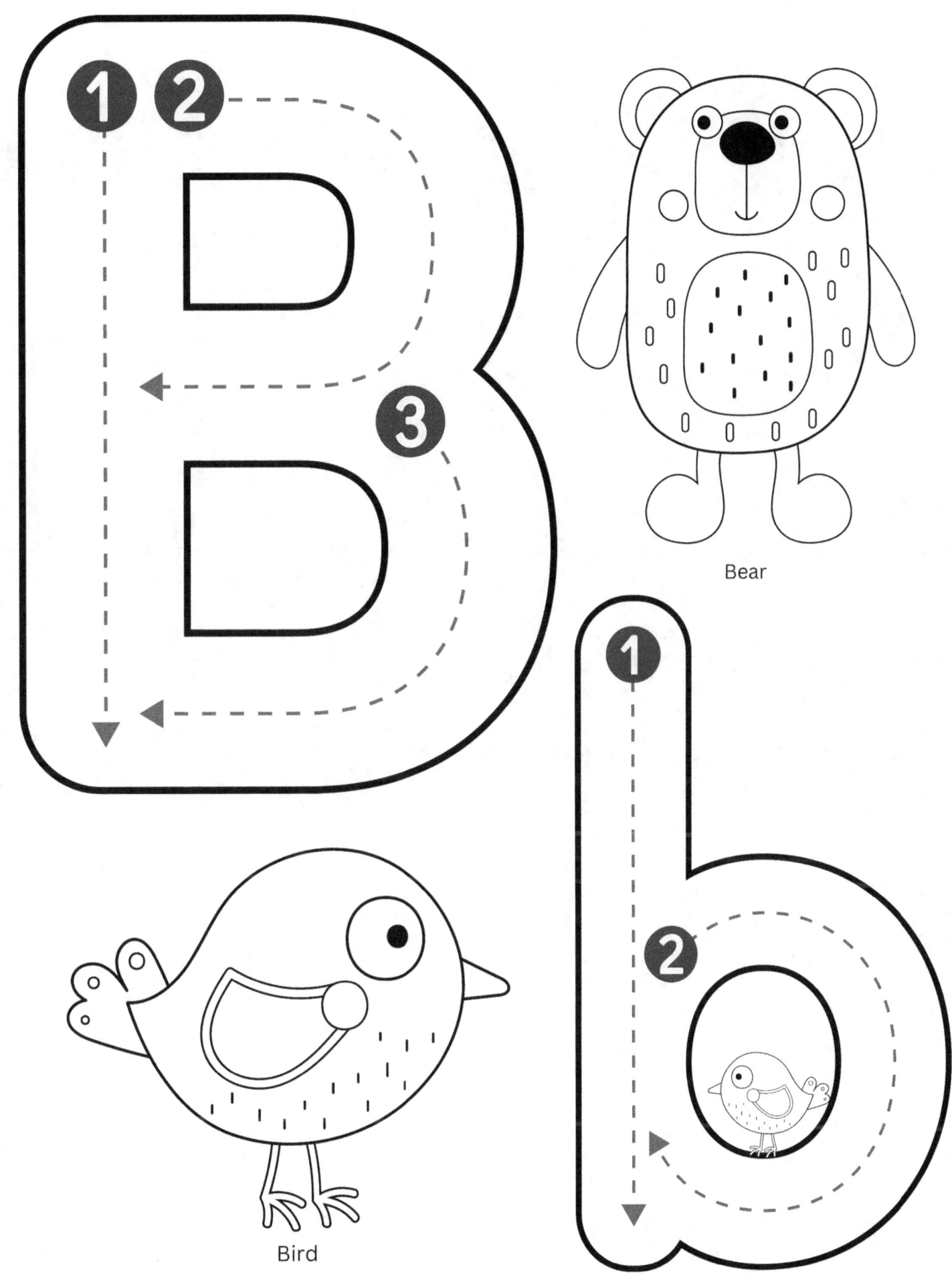

Bear

Bird

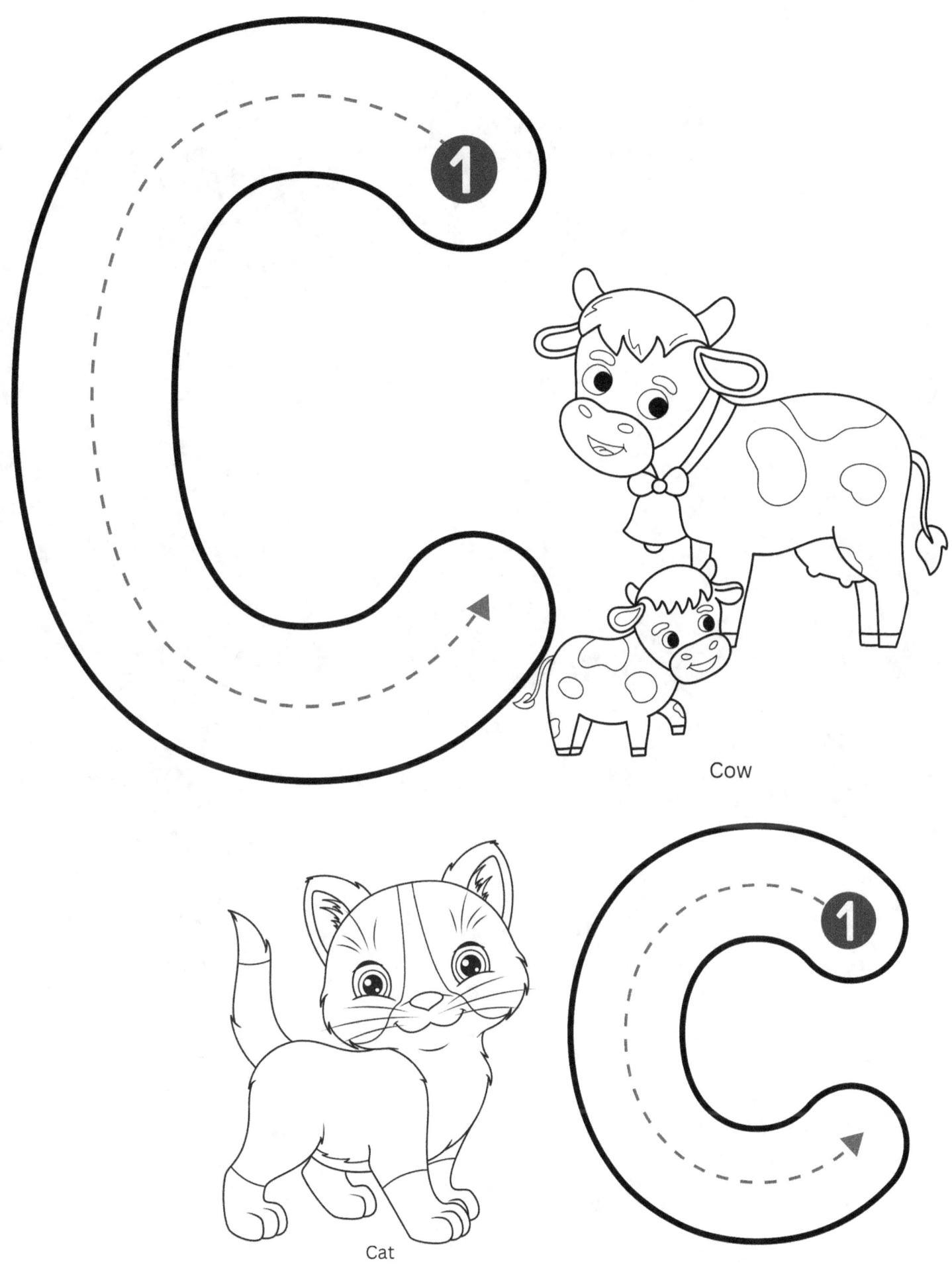

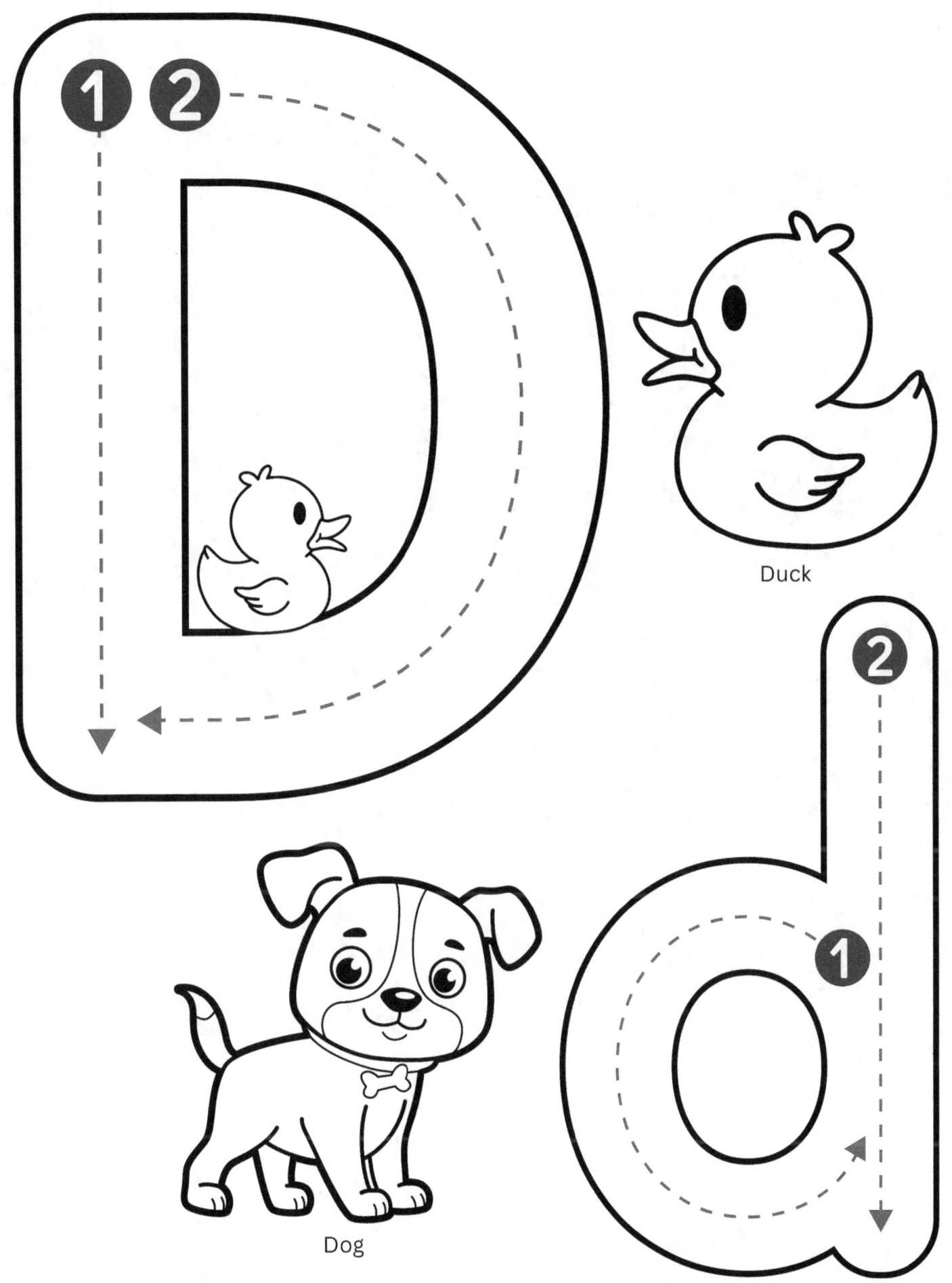

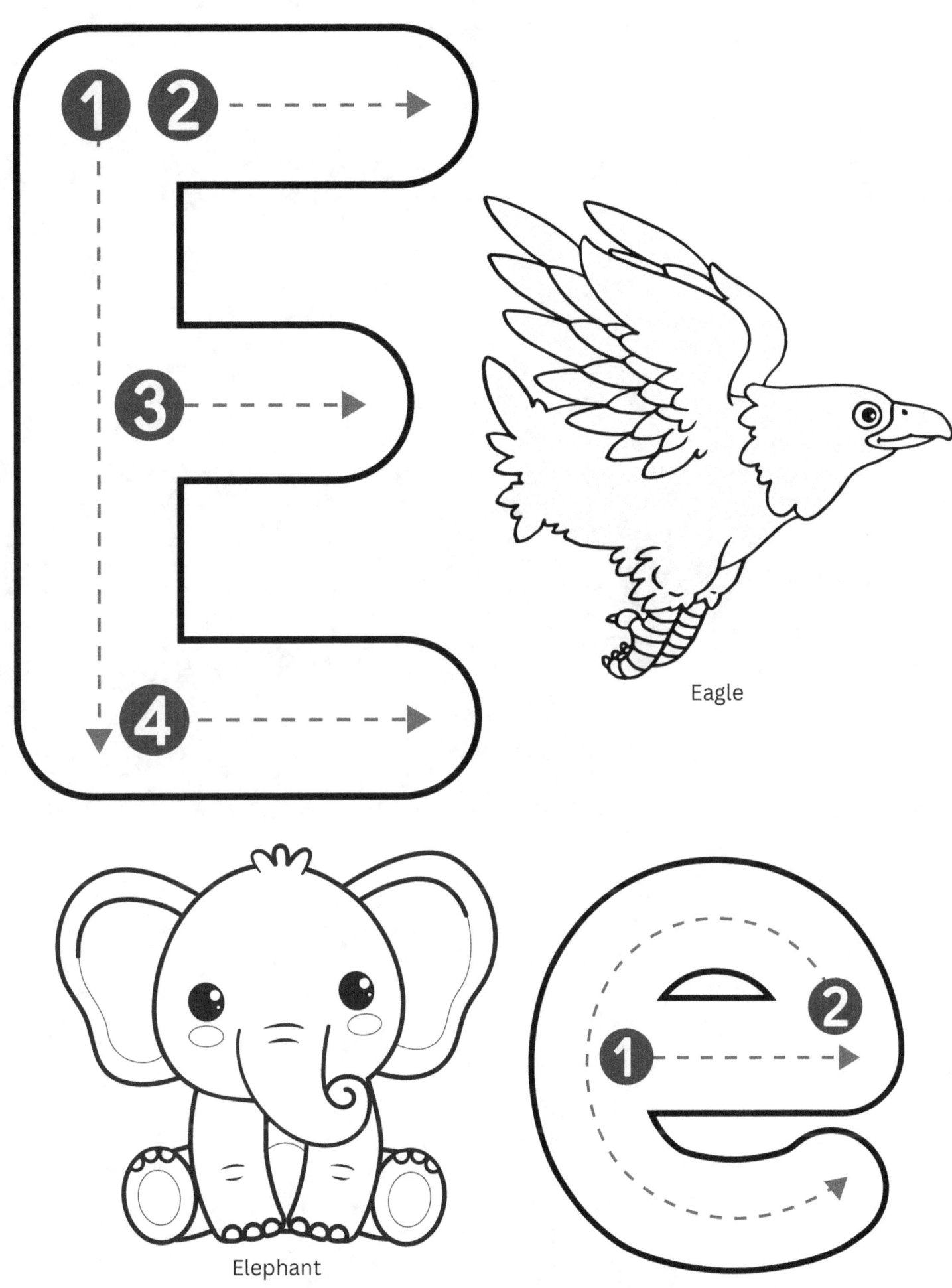

Eagle

Elephant

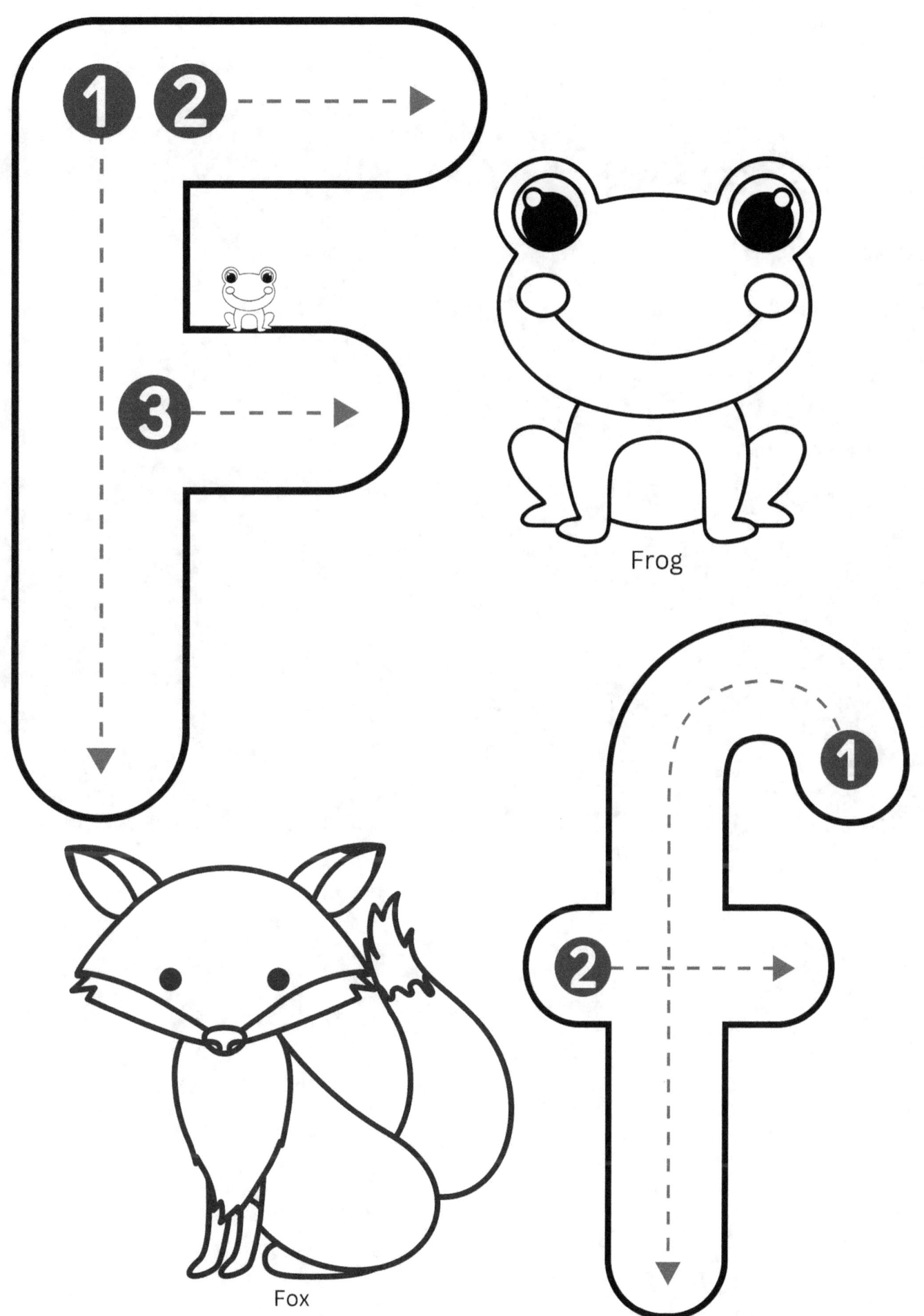

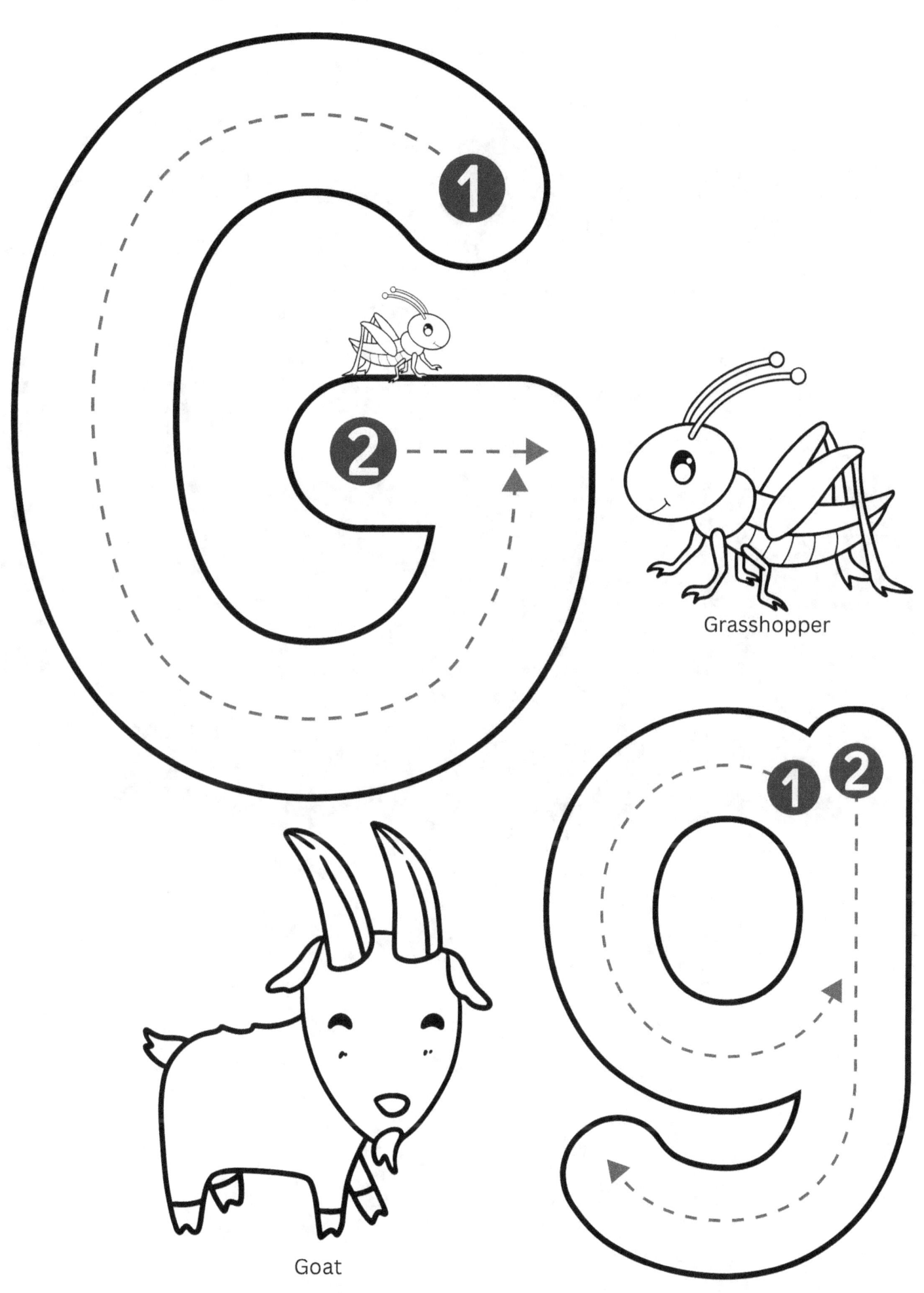

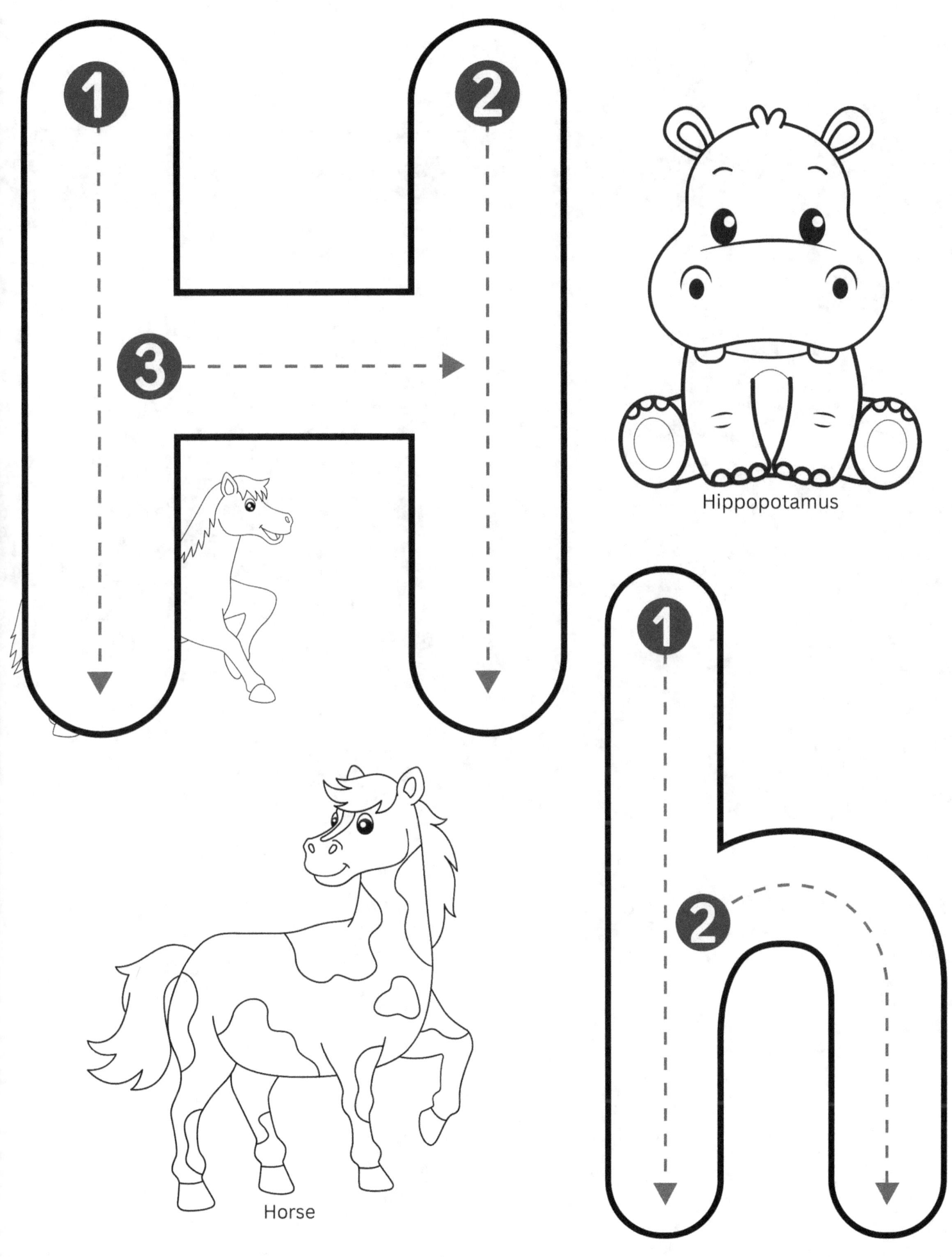

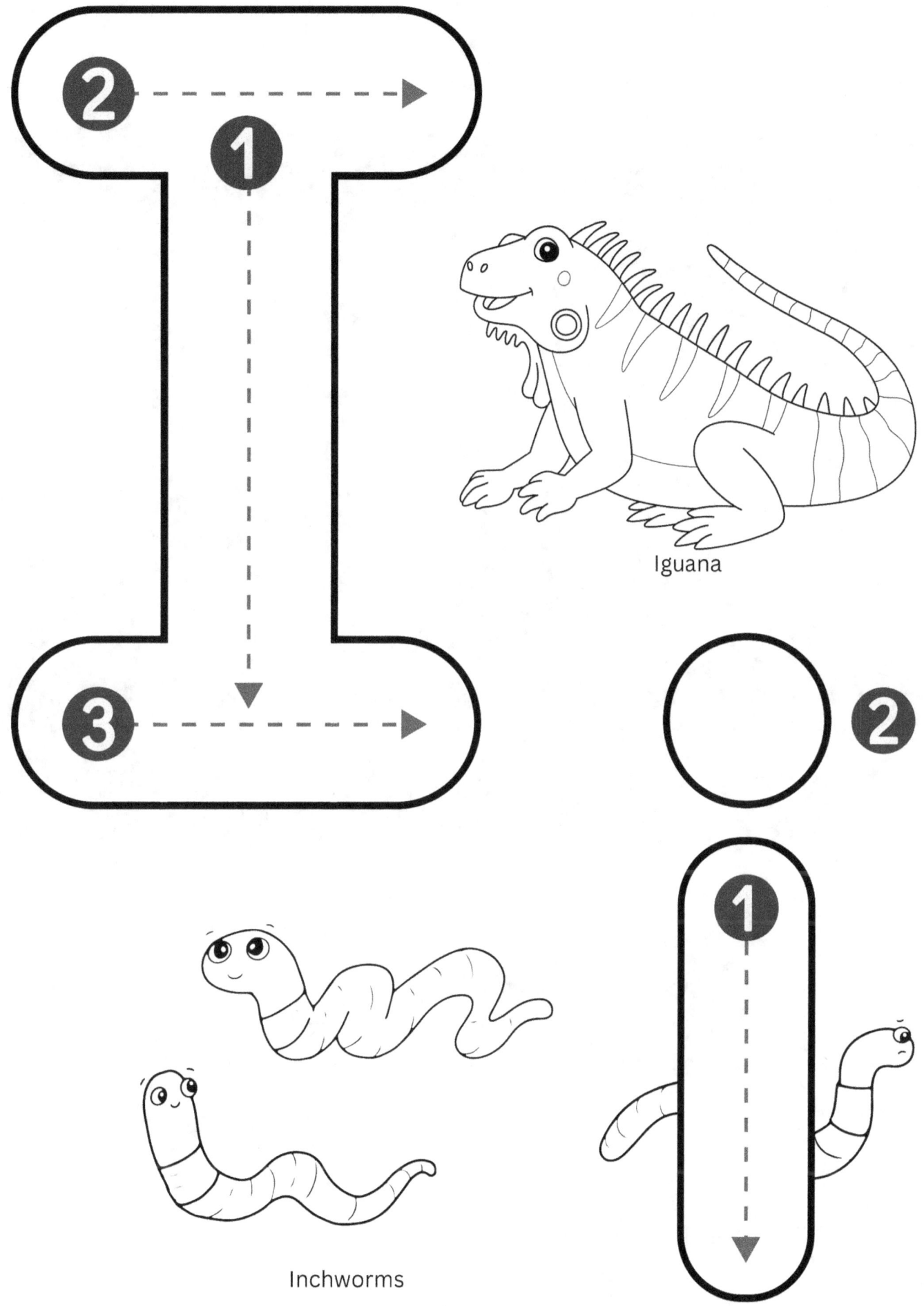

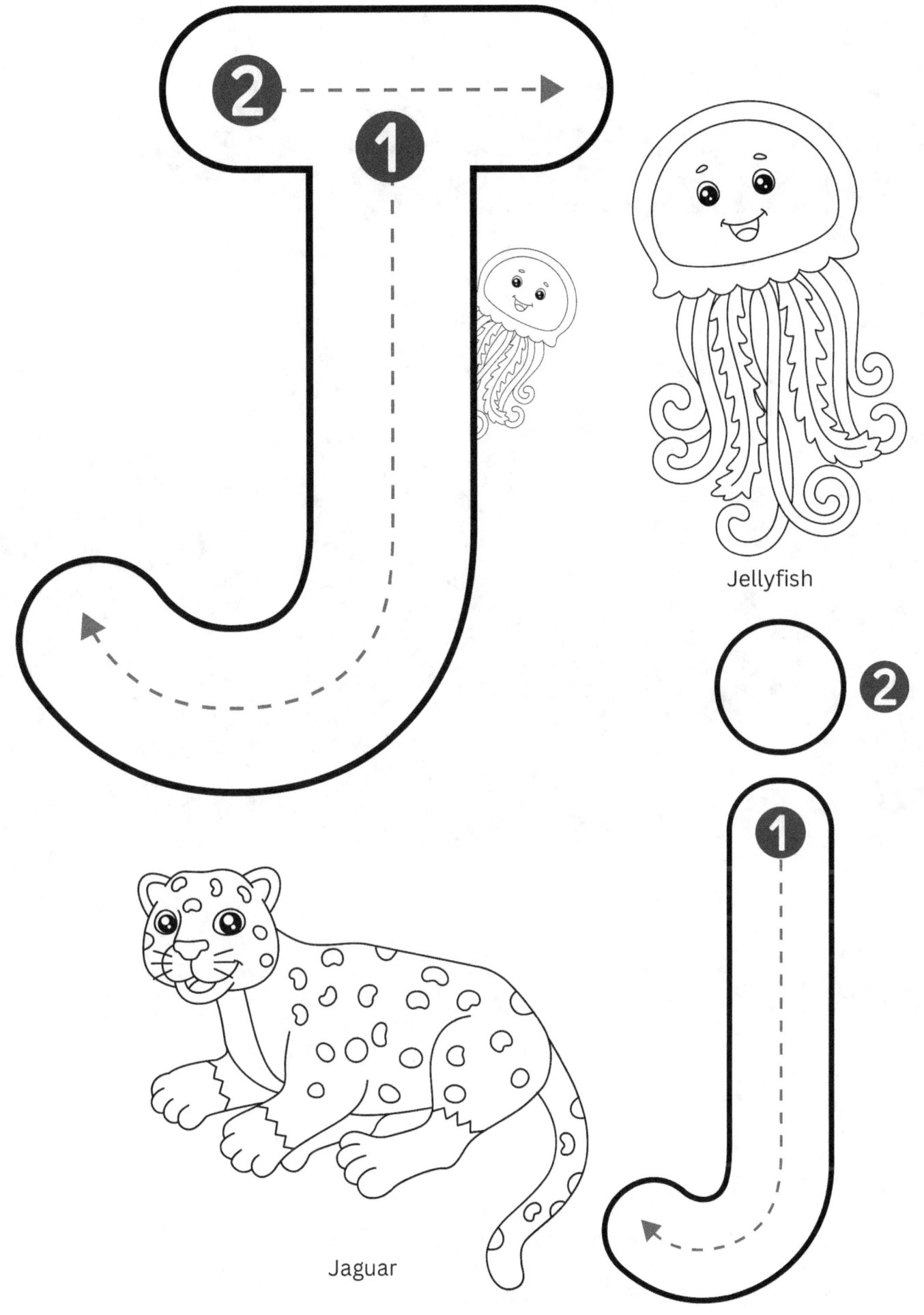

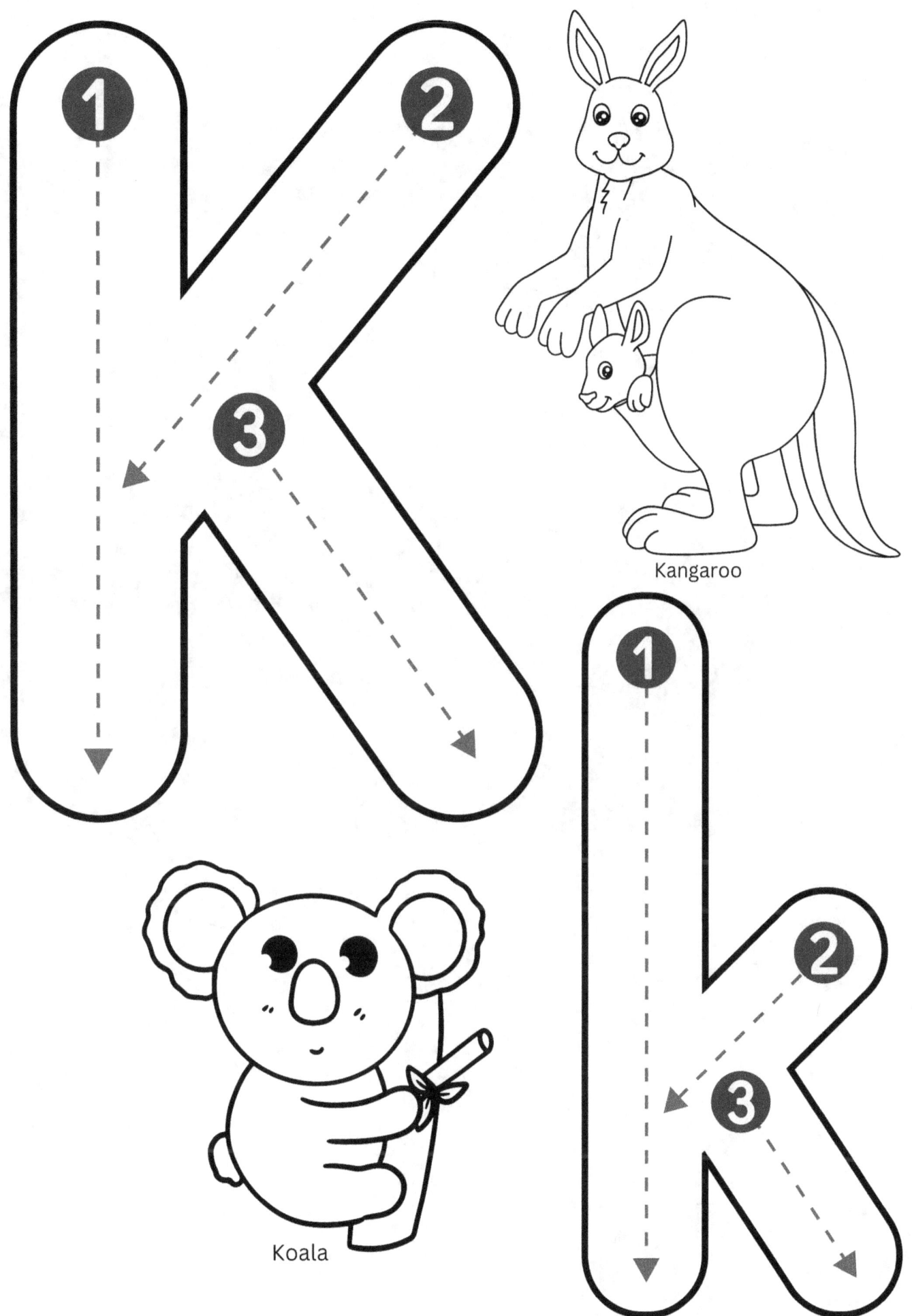

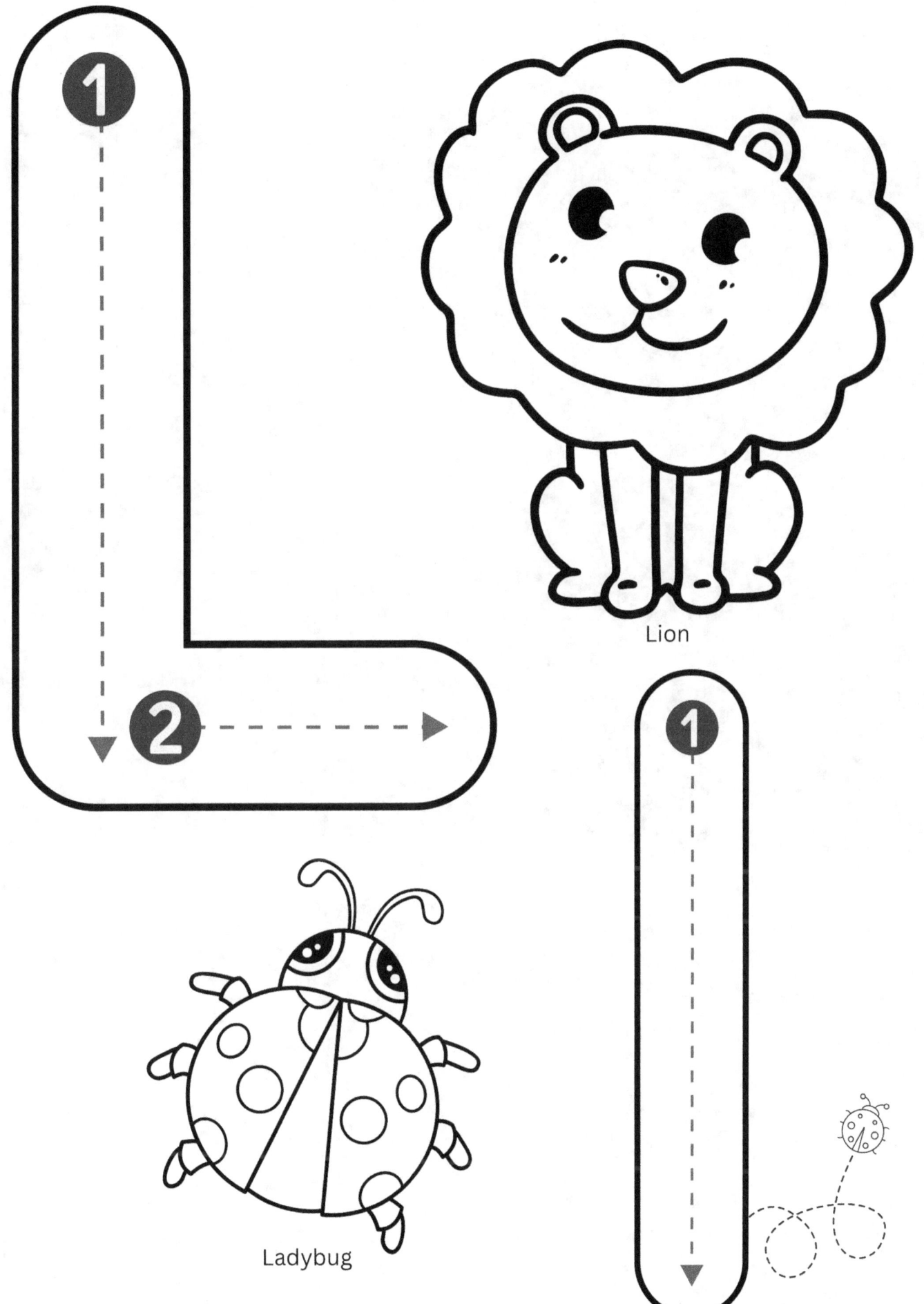

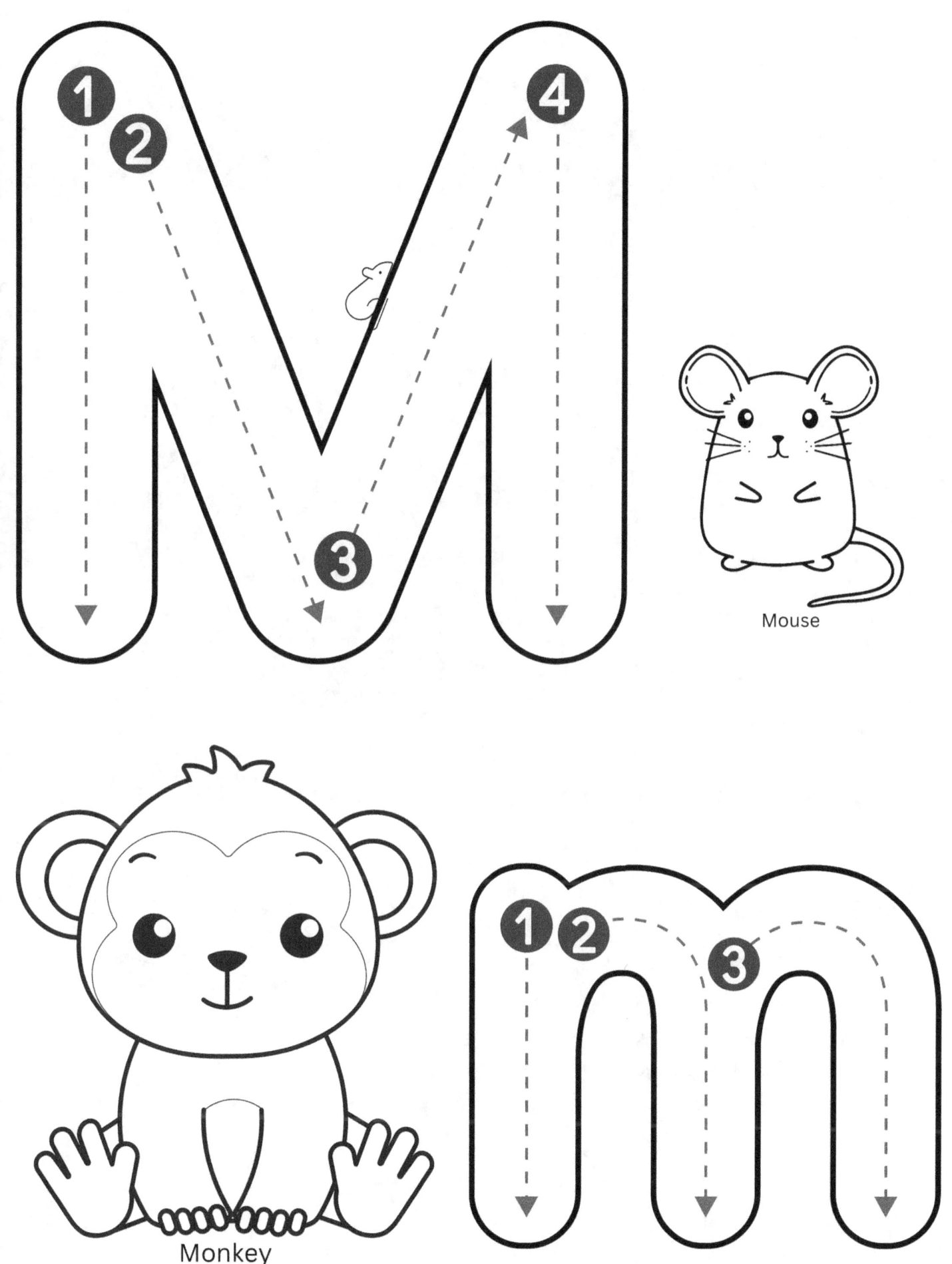

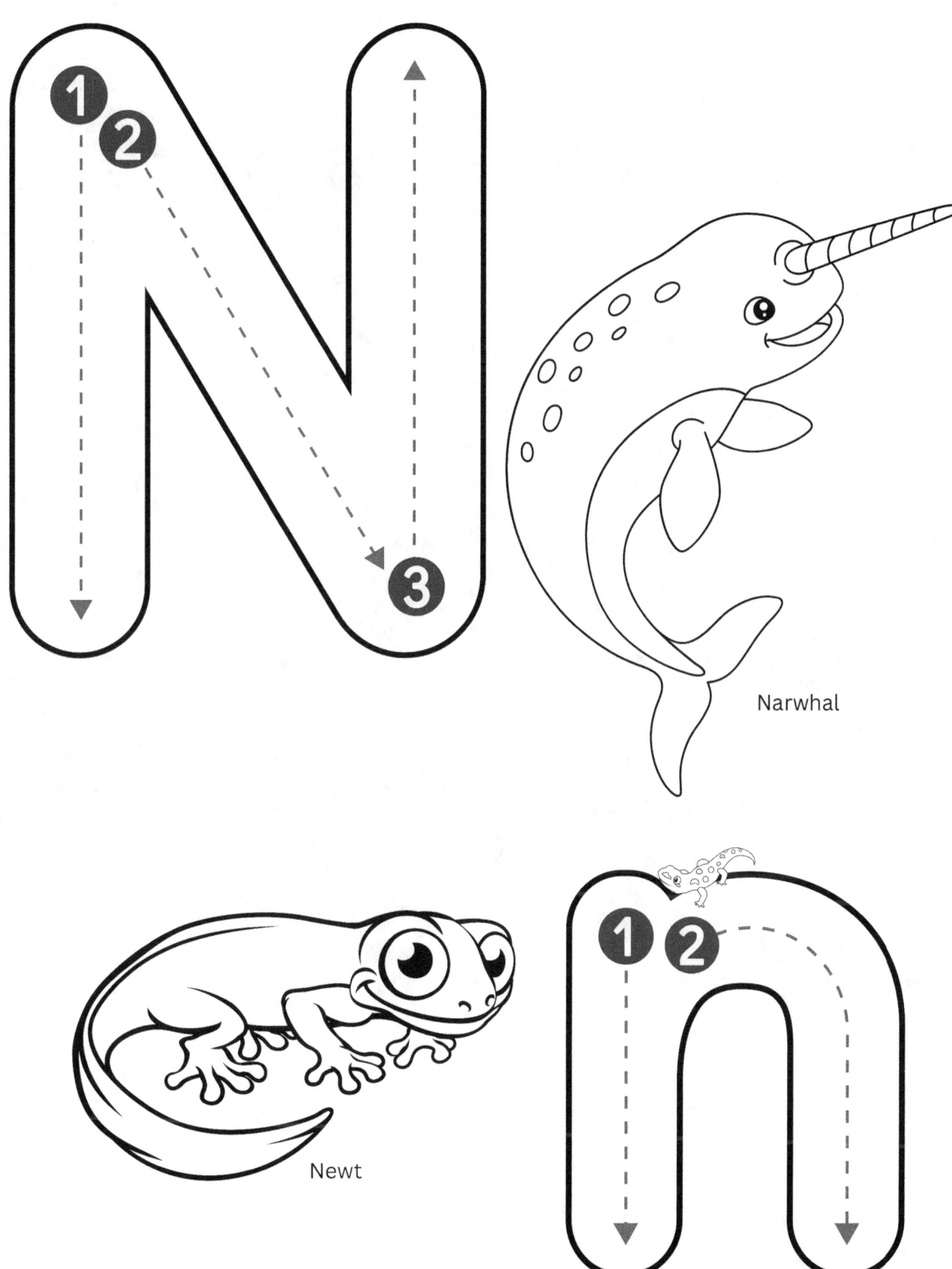

Narwhal

Newt

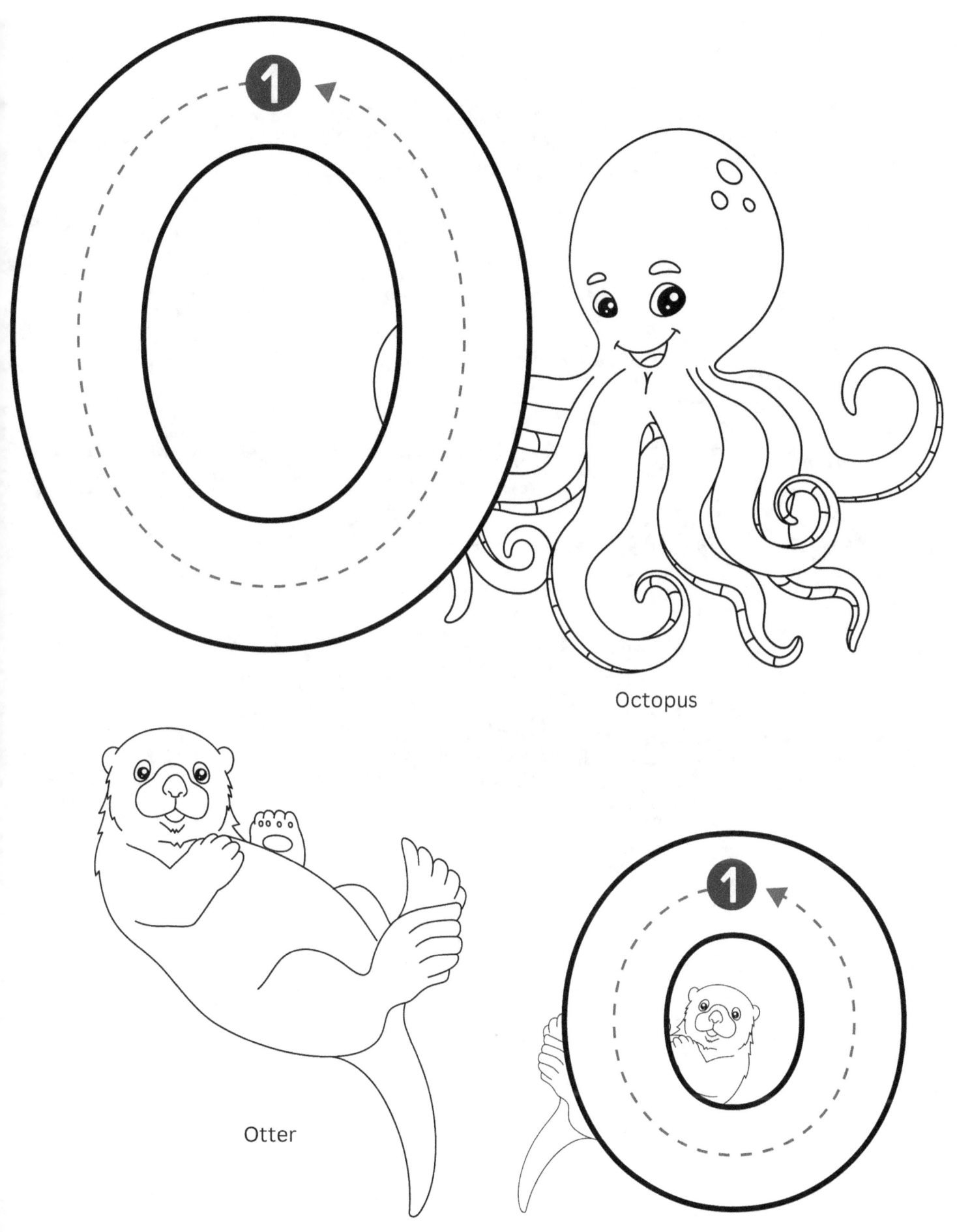

Octopus

Otter

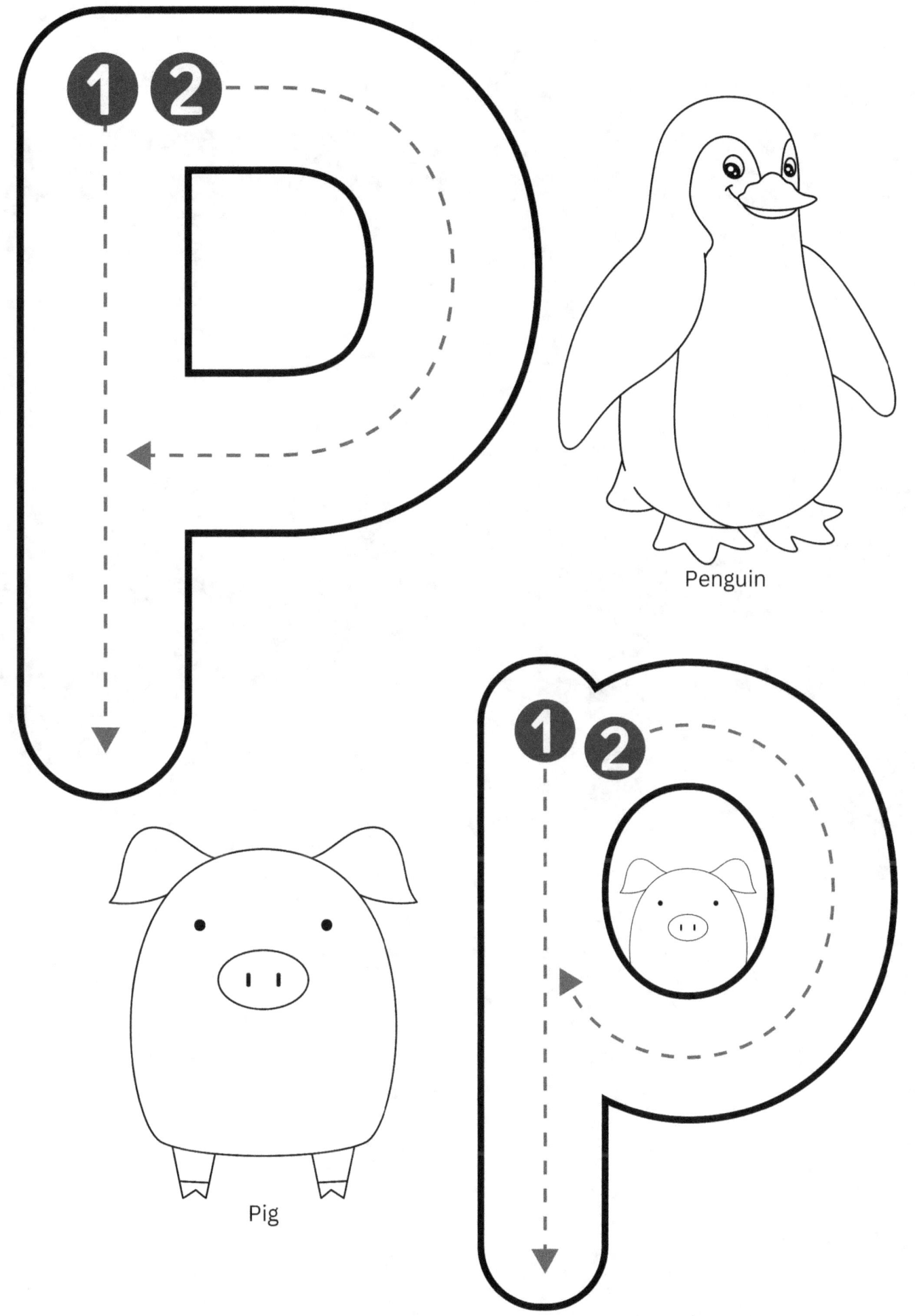

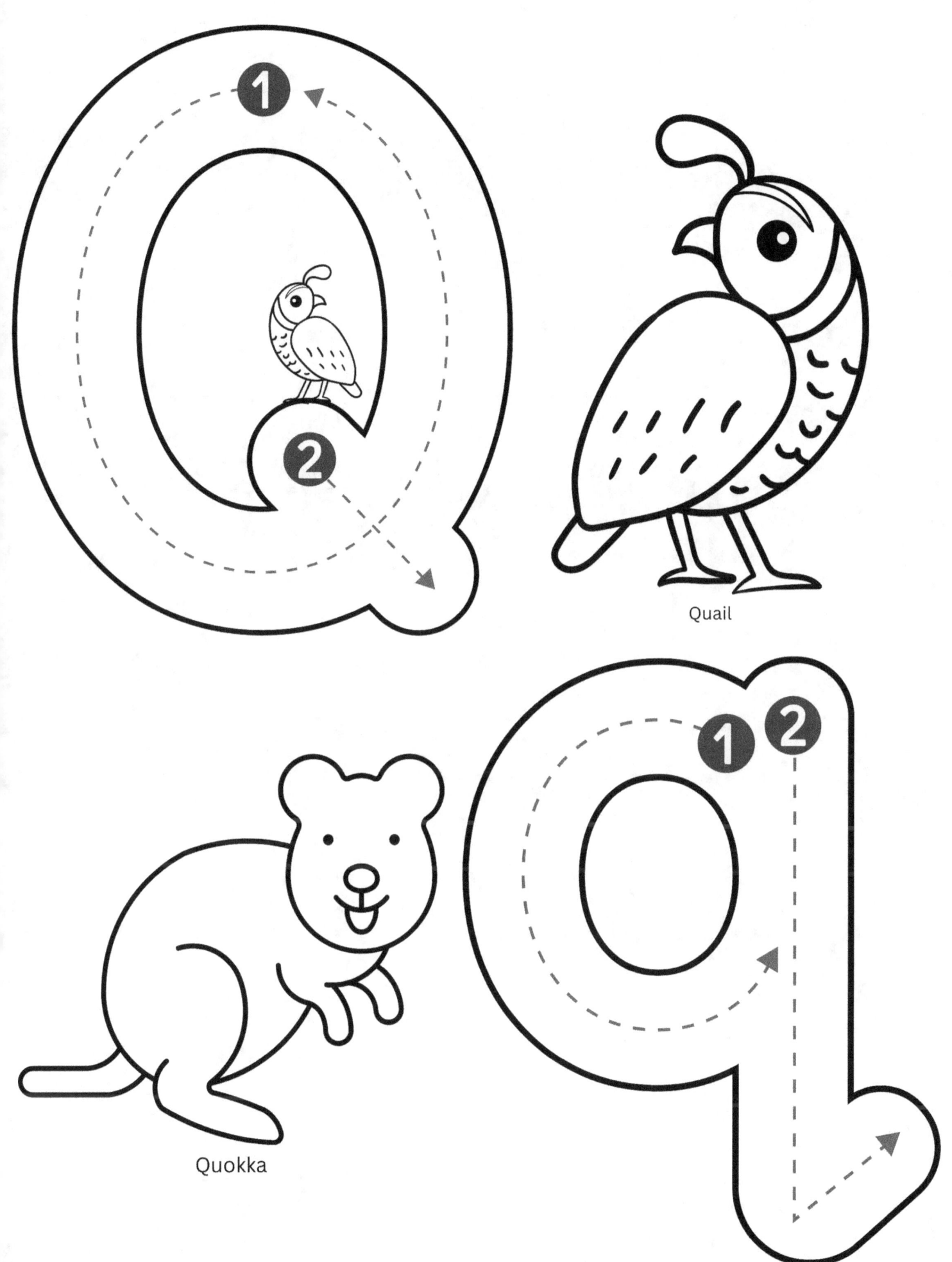

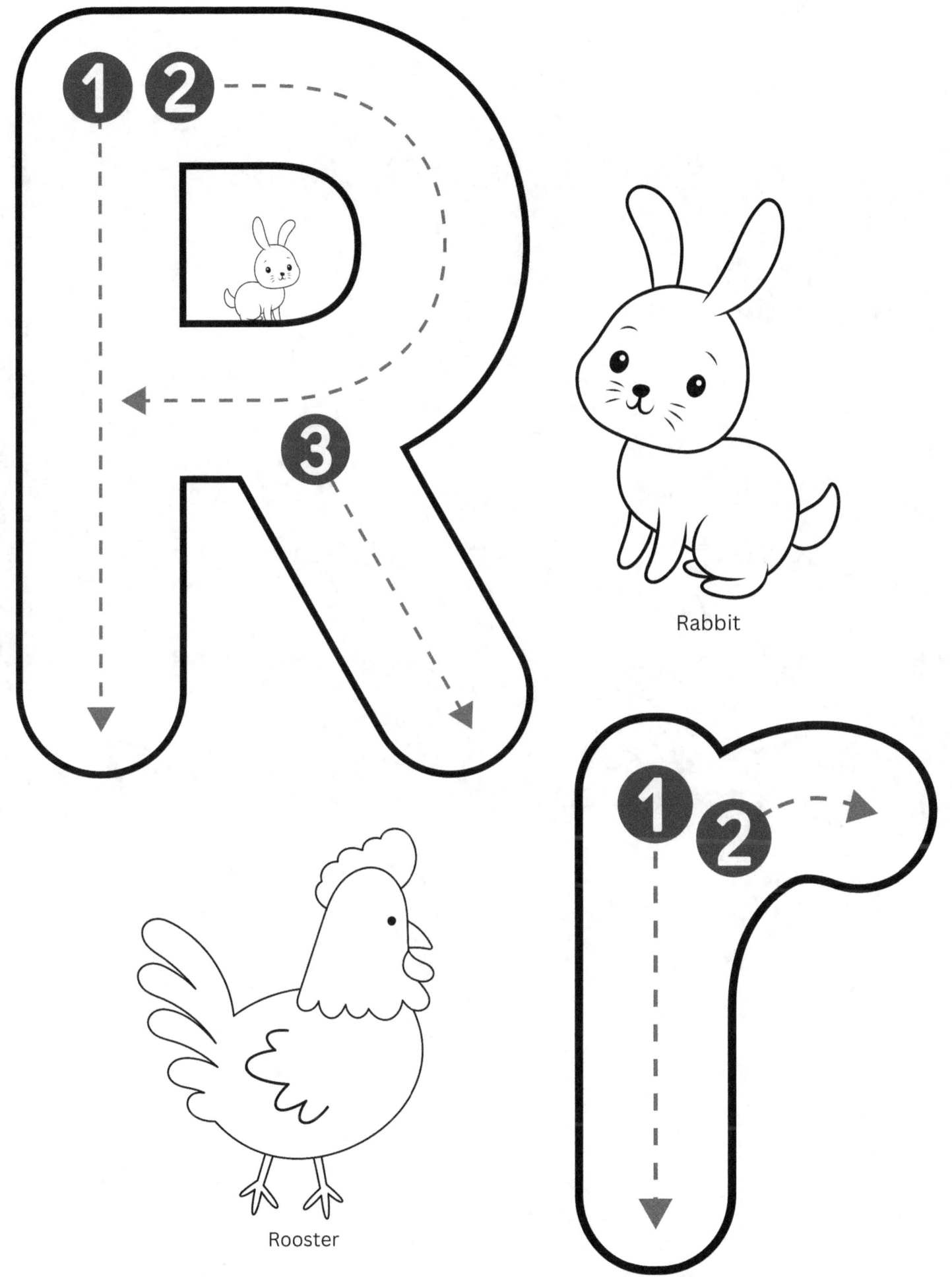

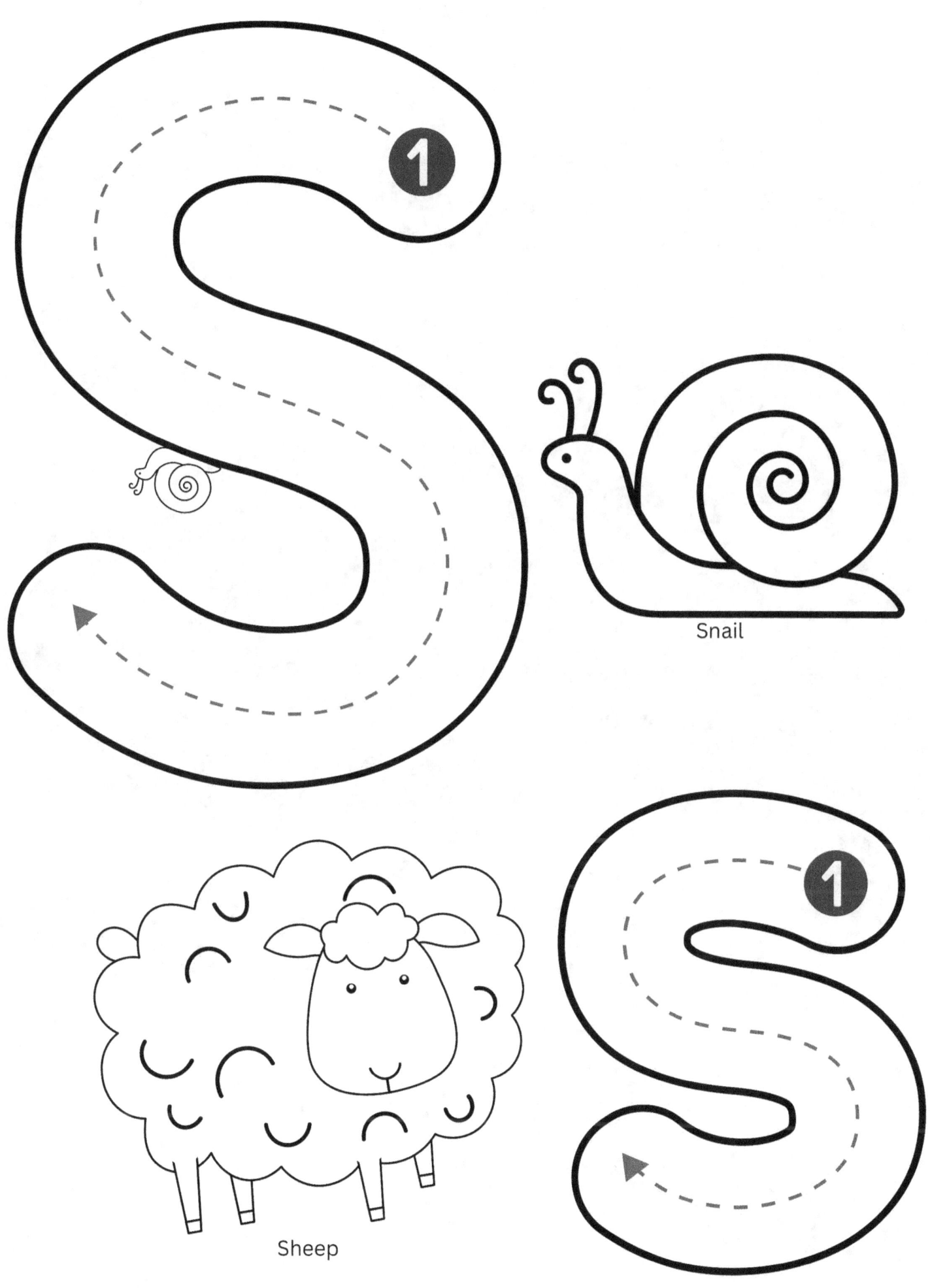

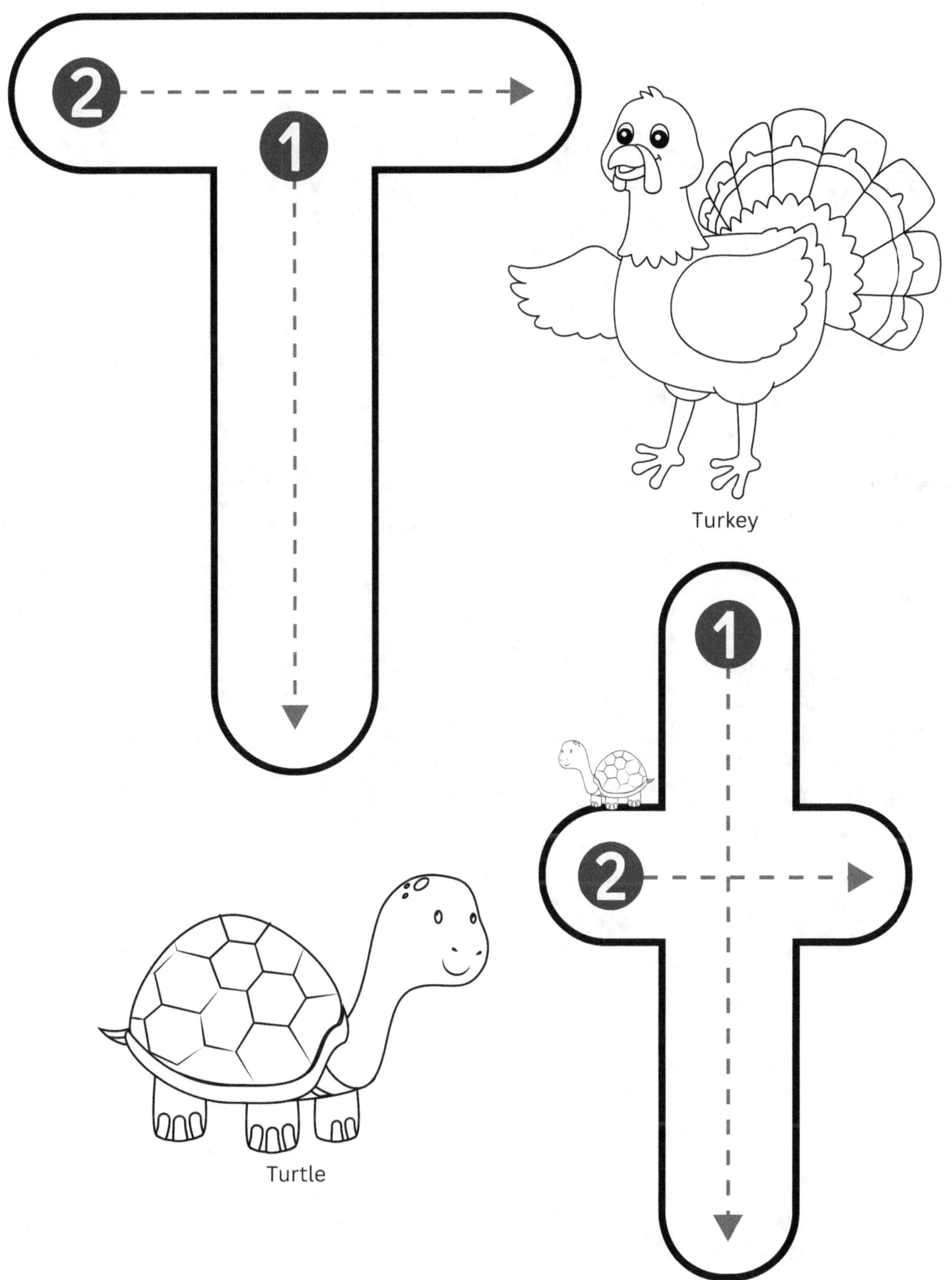

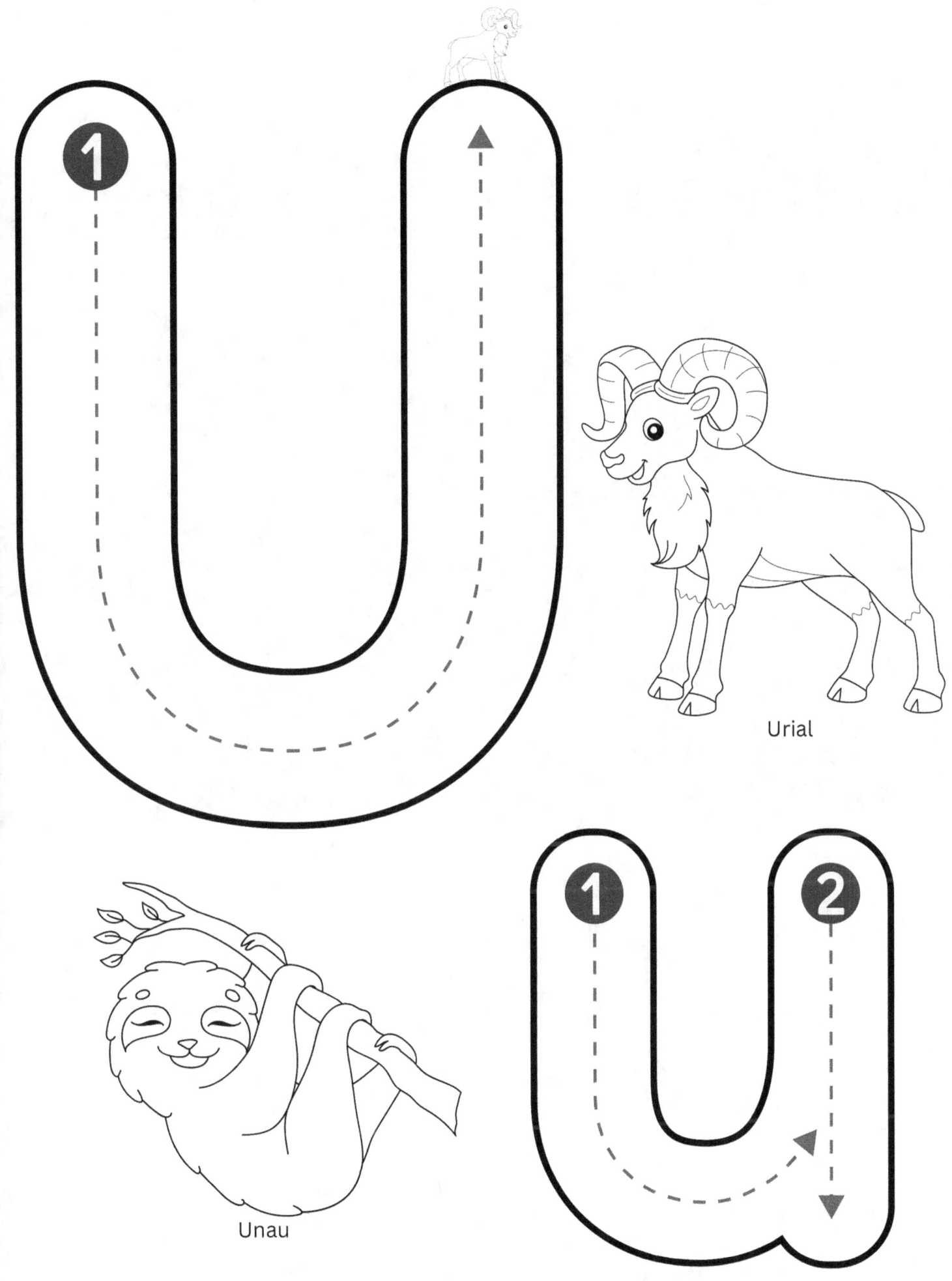

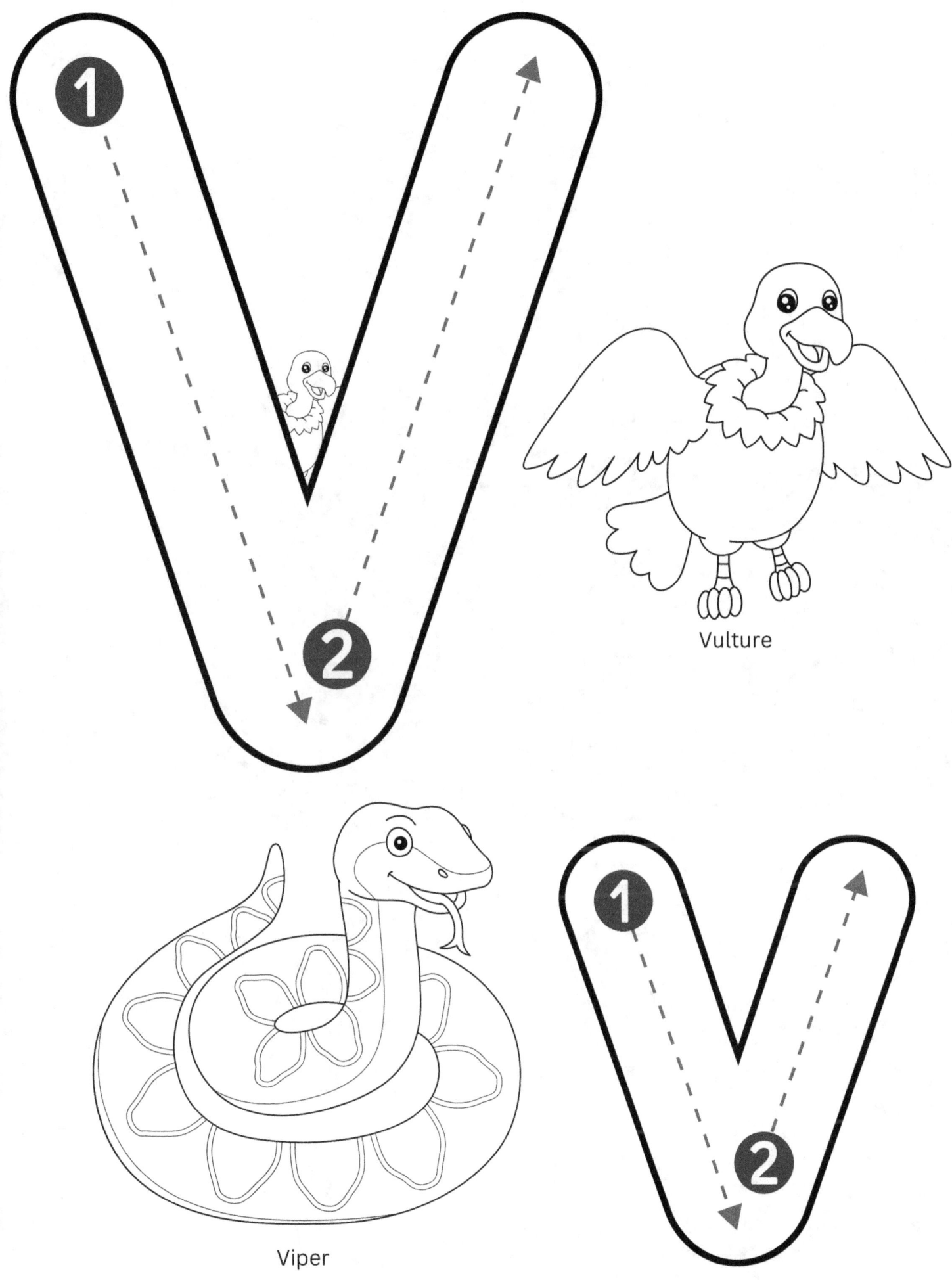

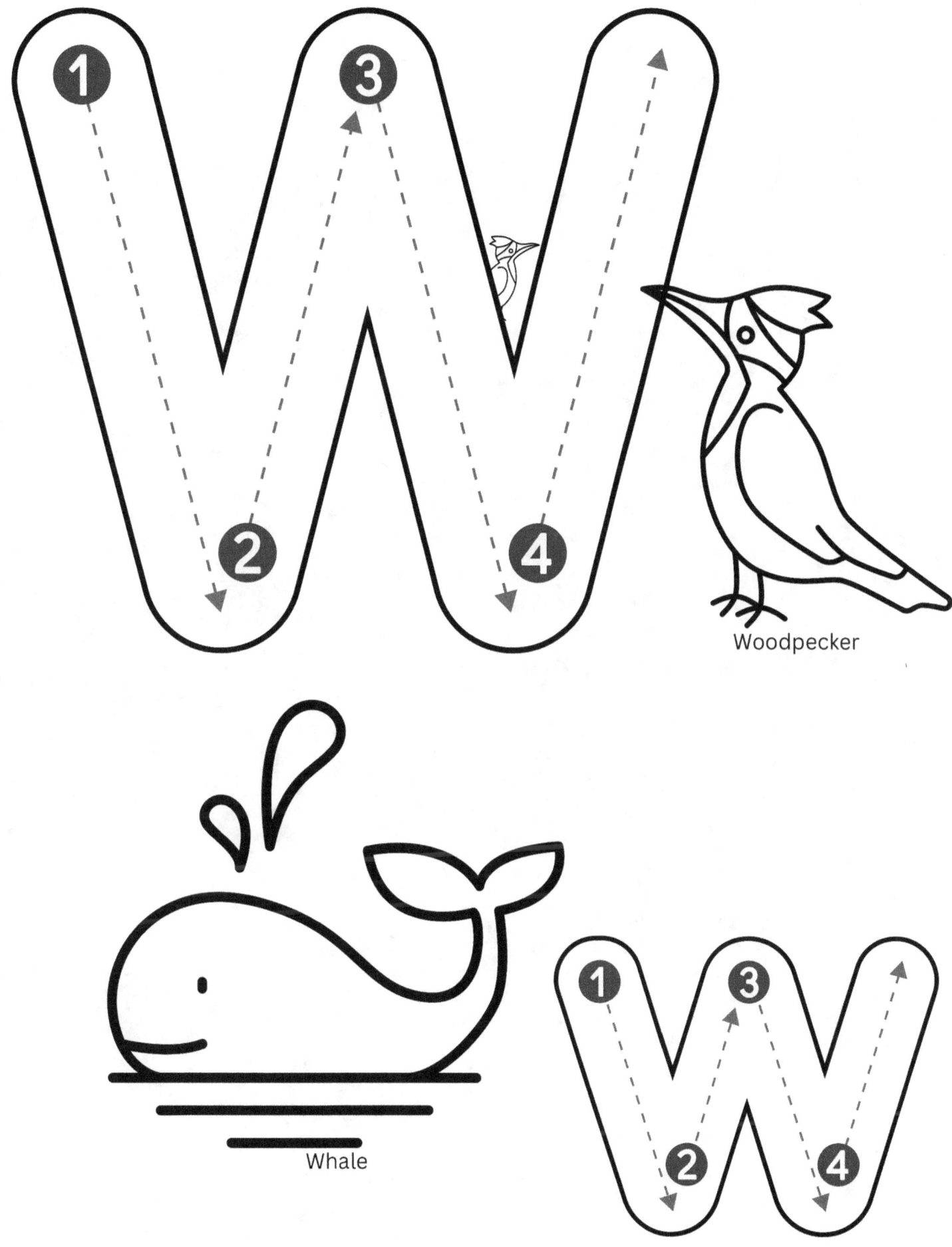

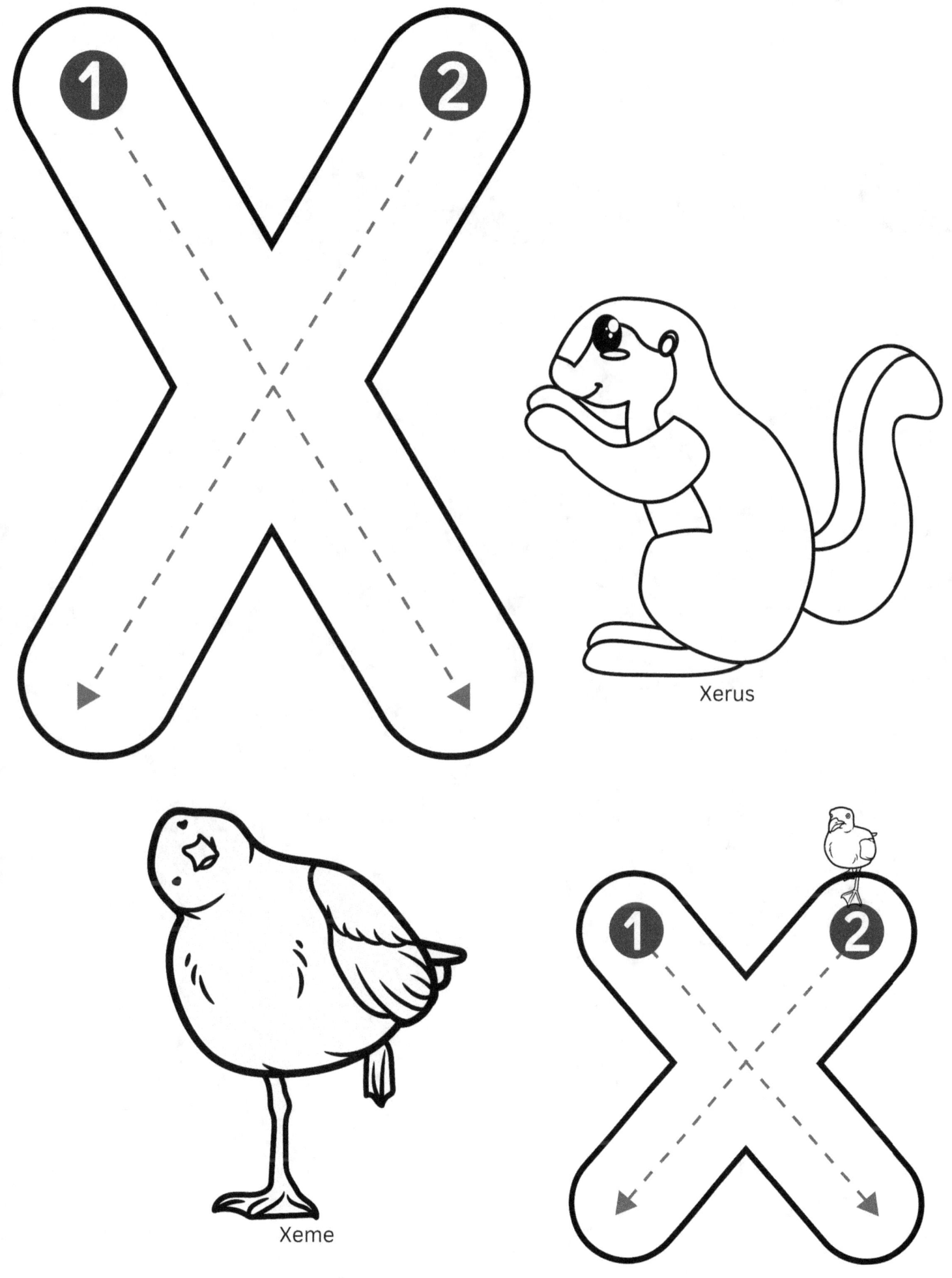

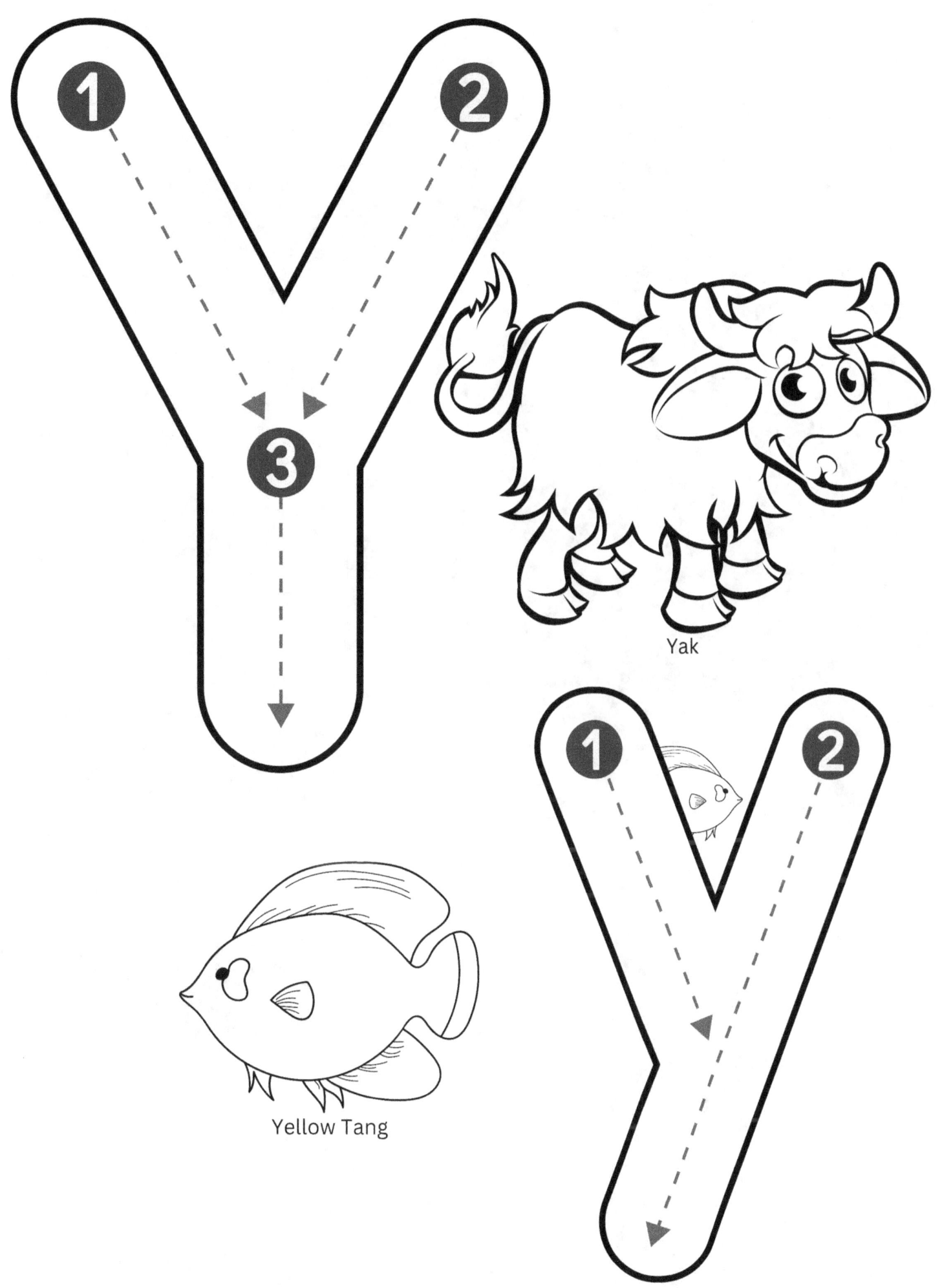

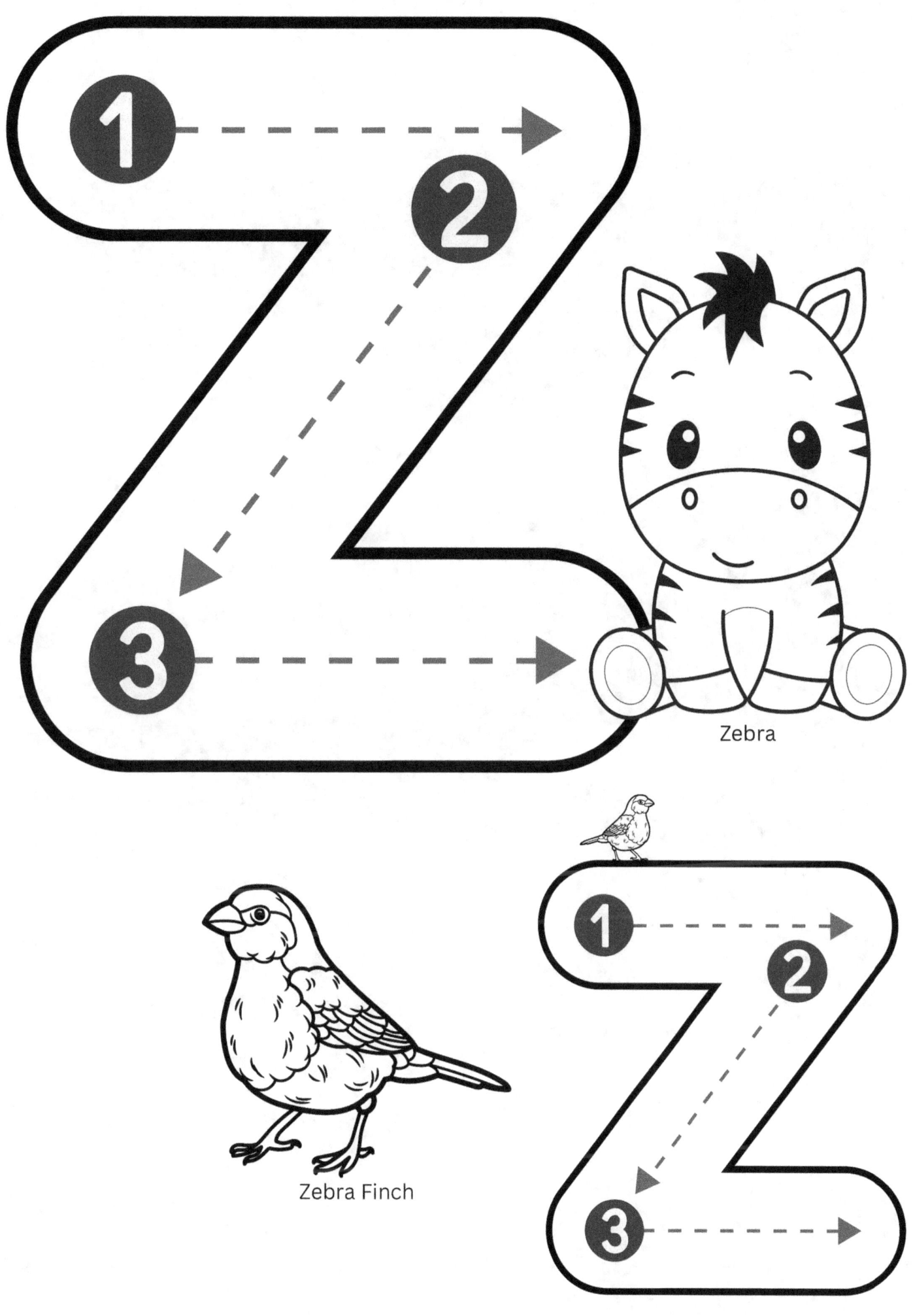

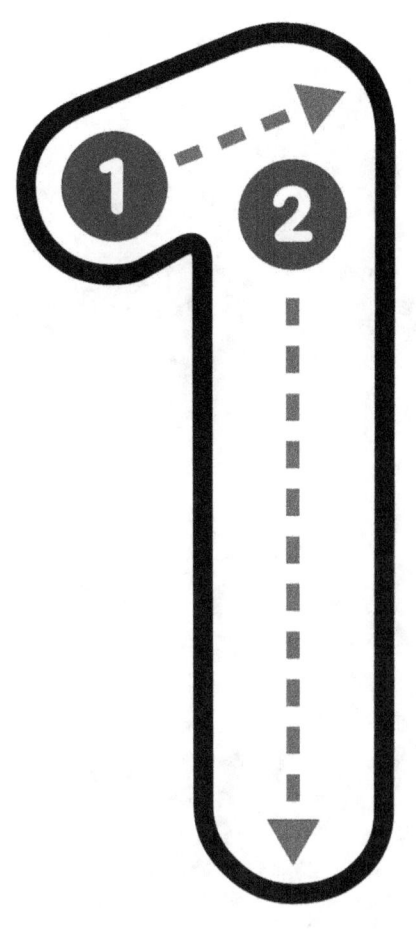
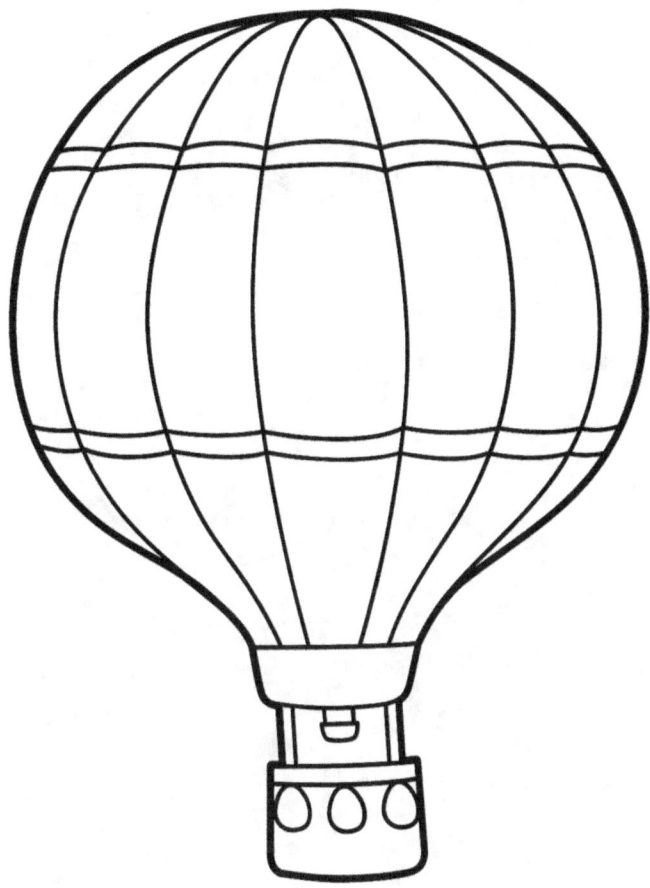
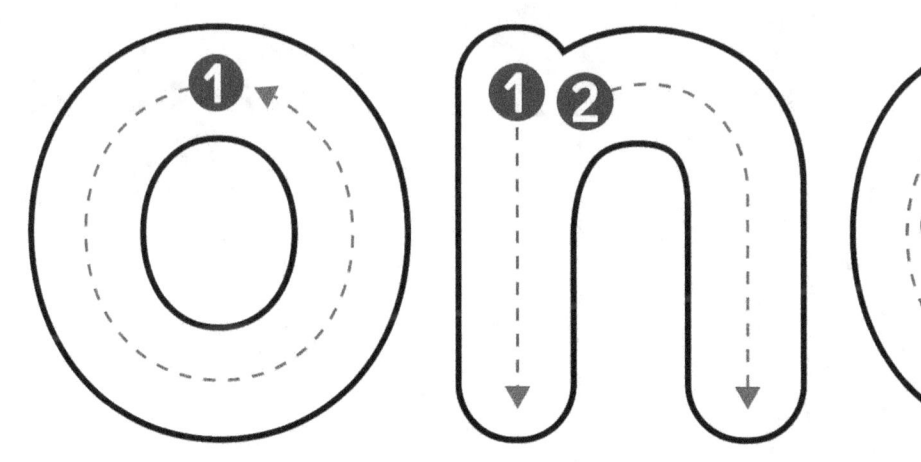

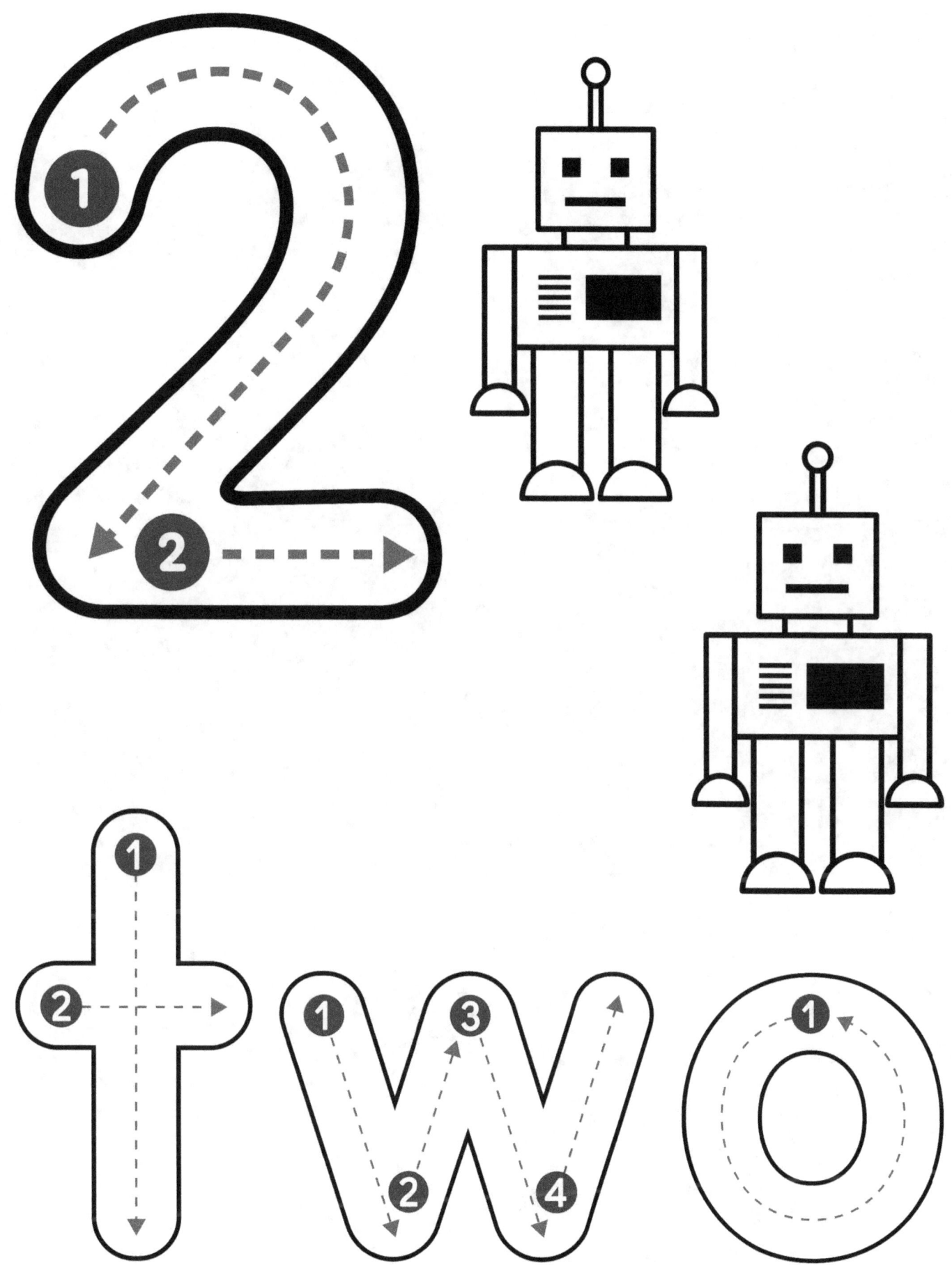

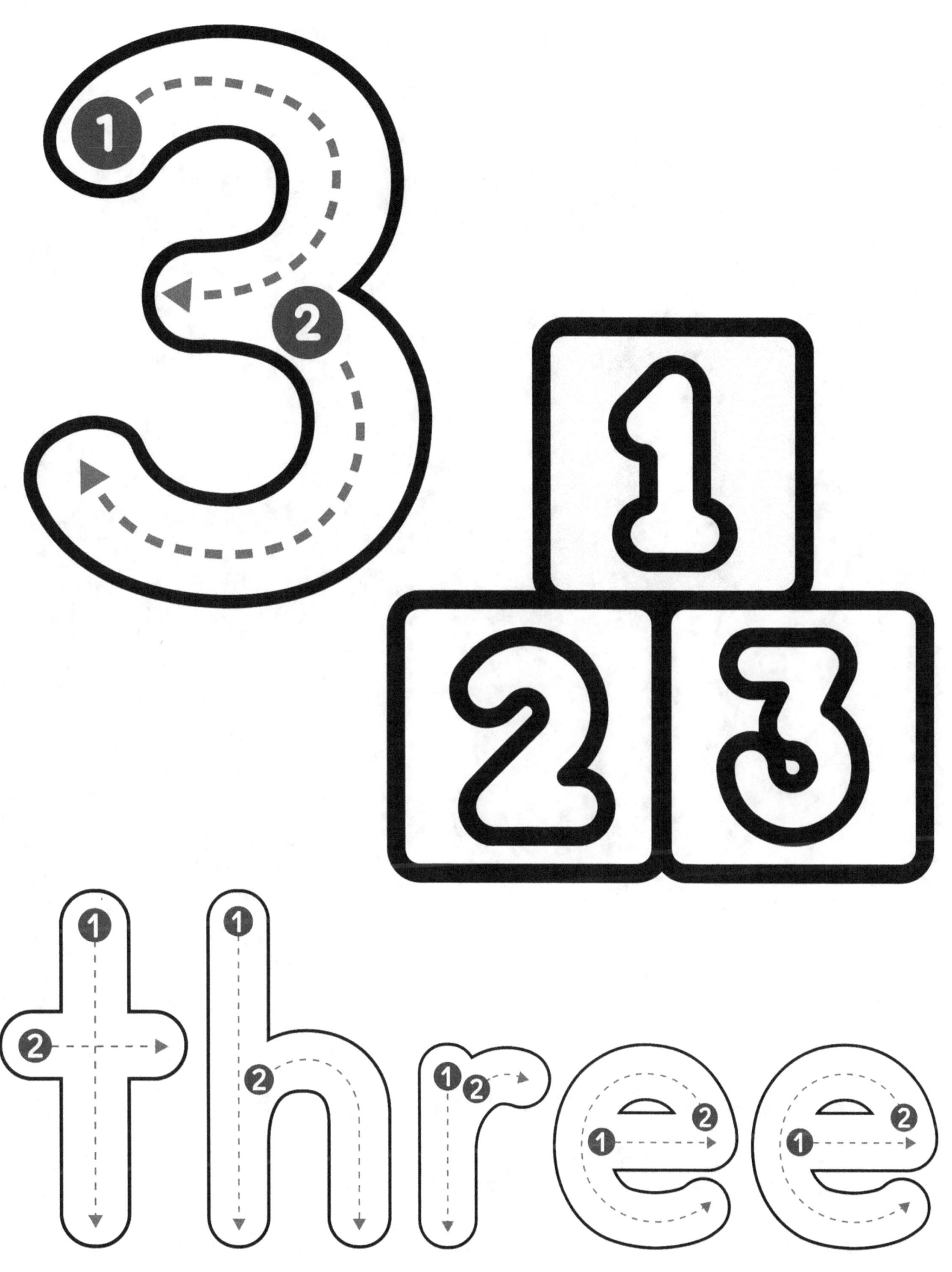

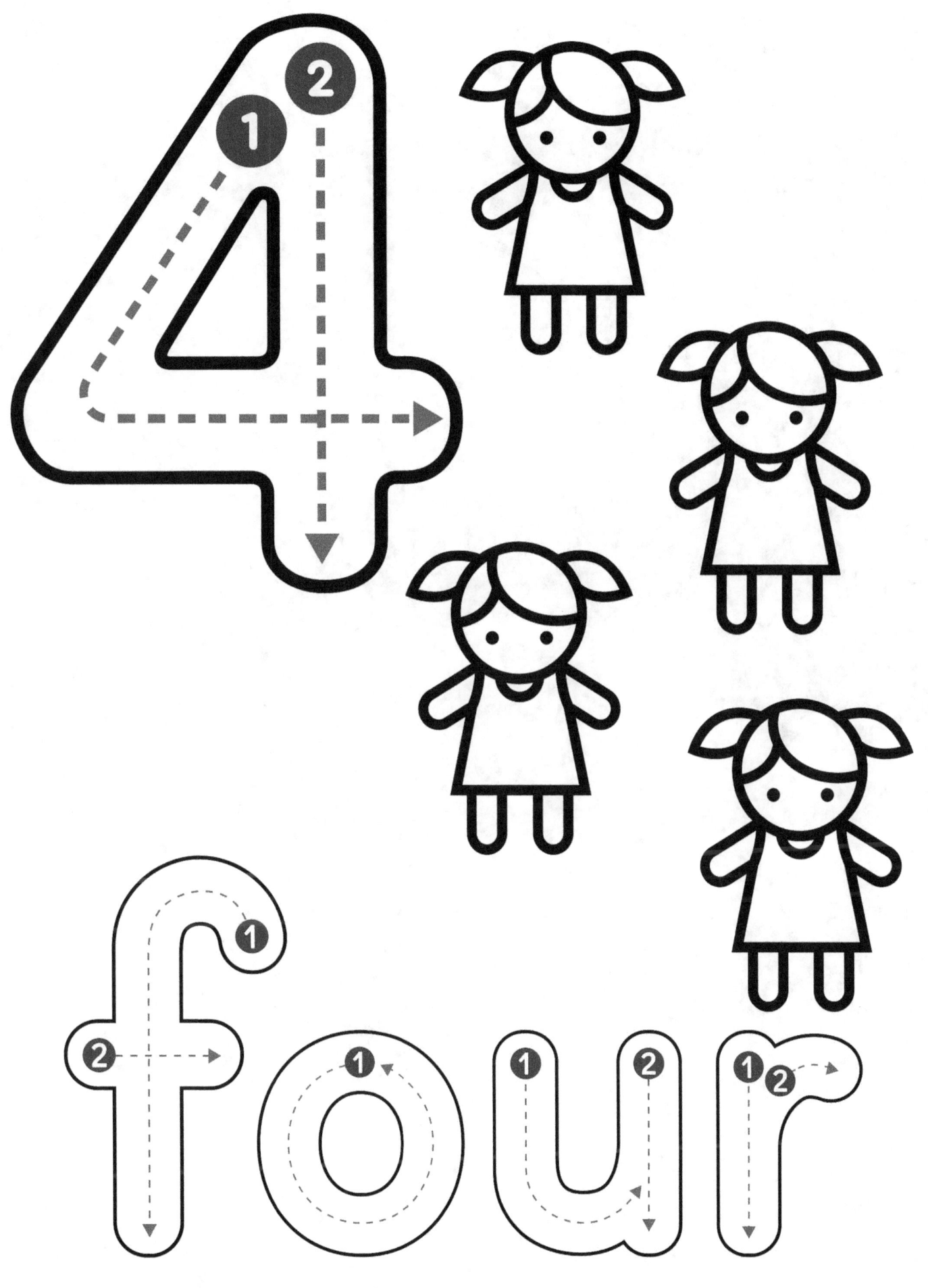

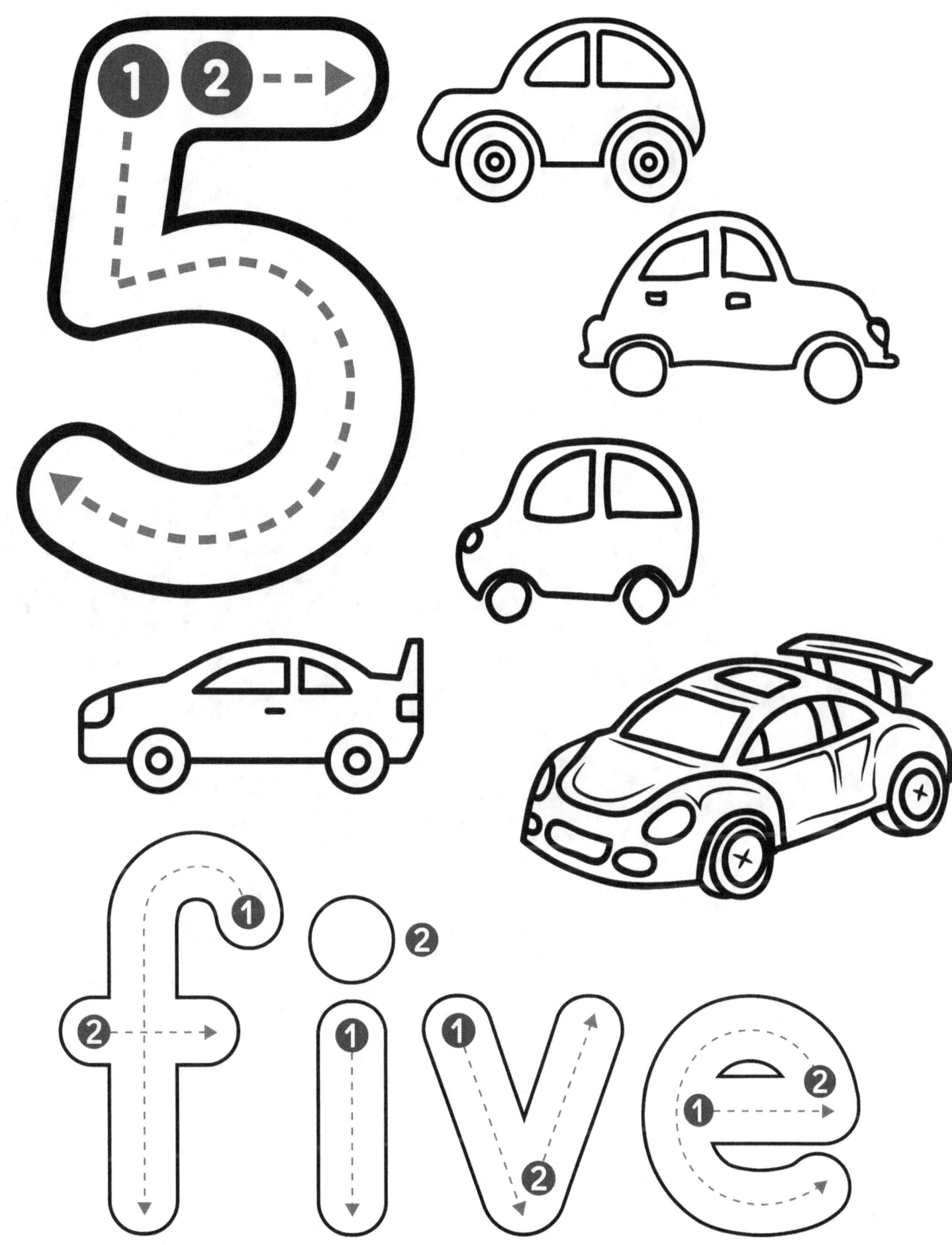

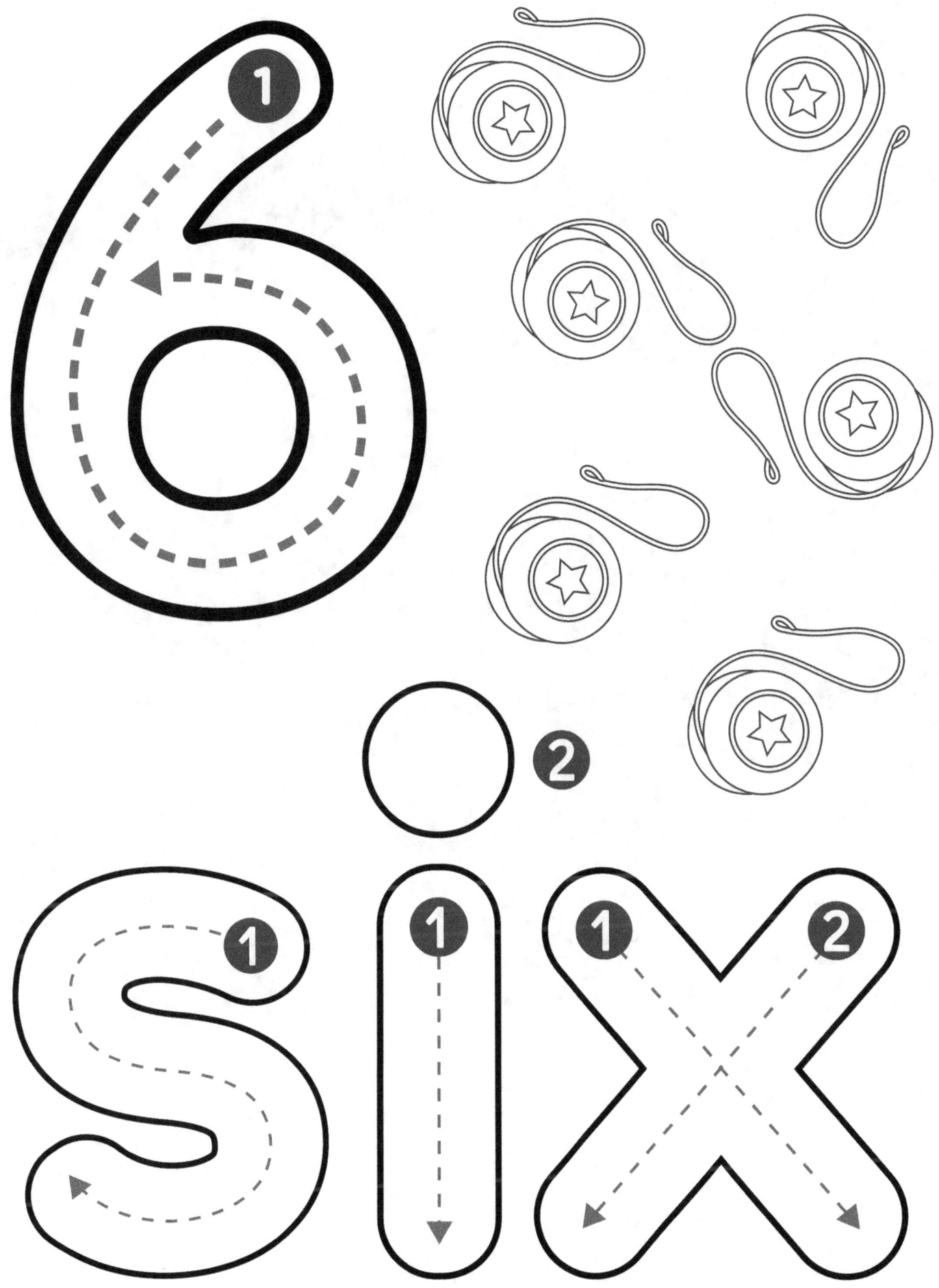

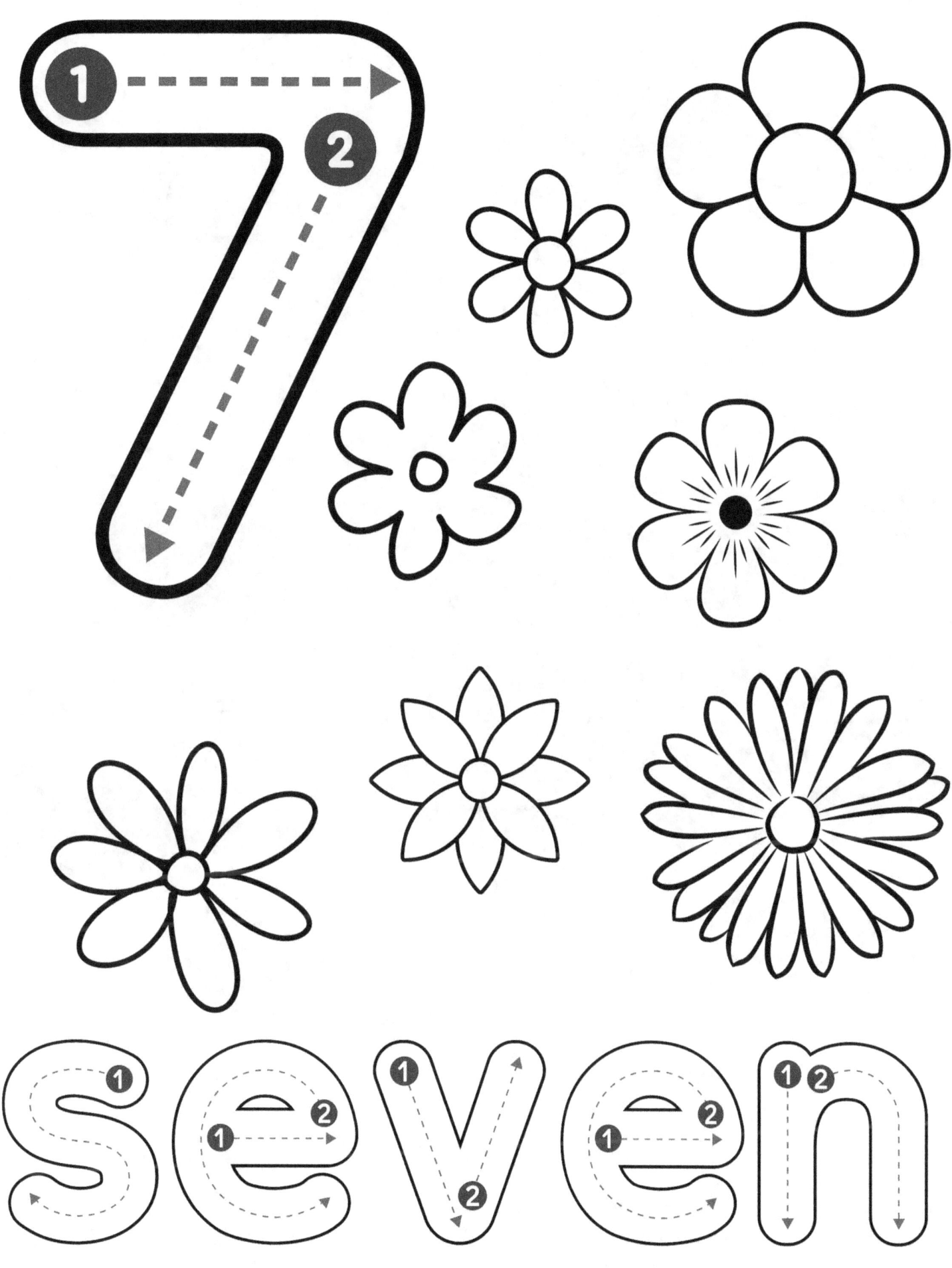

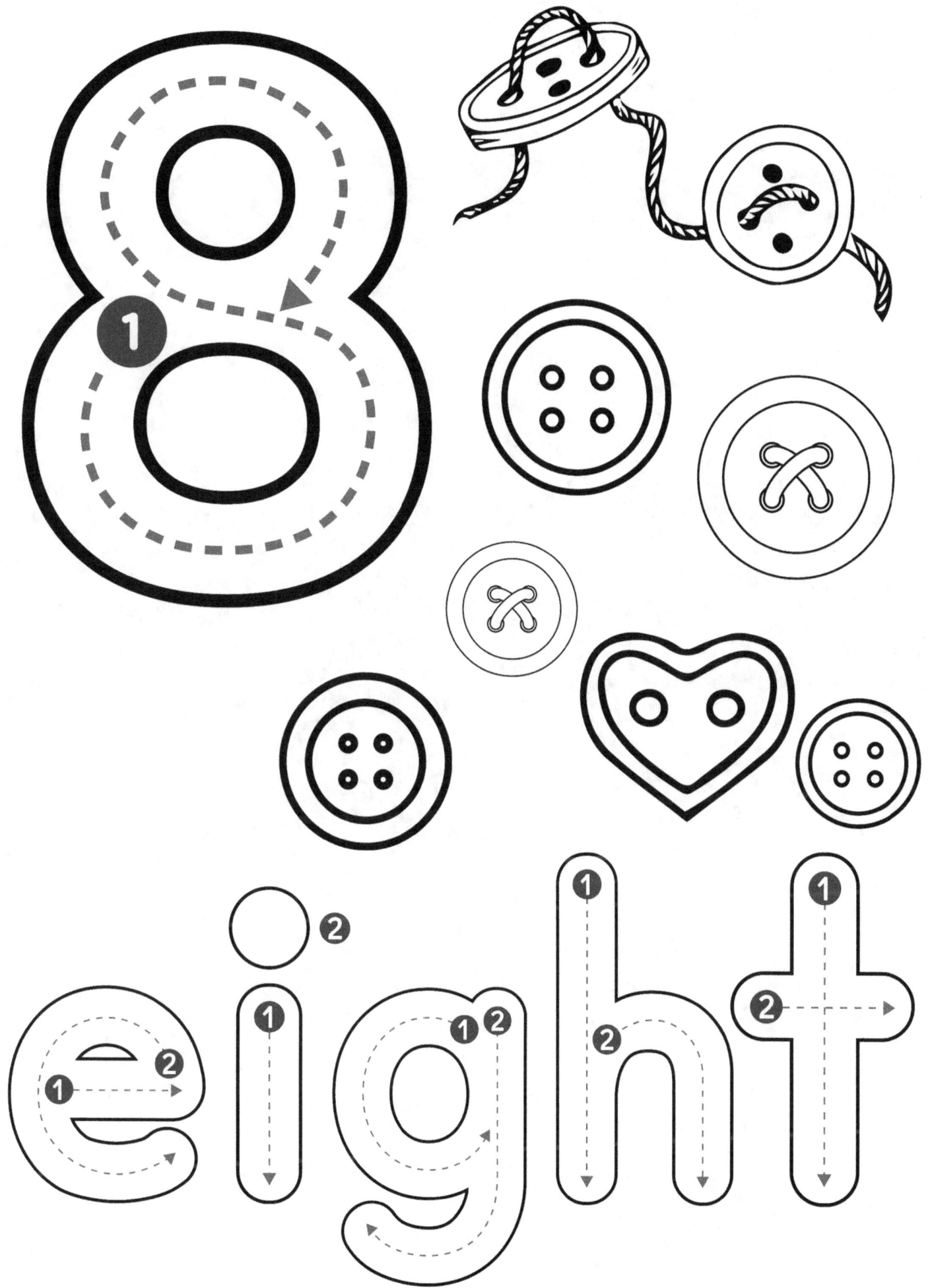

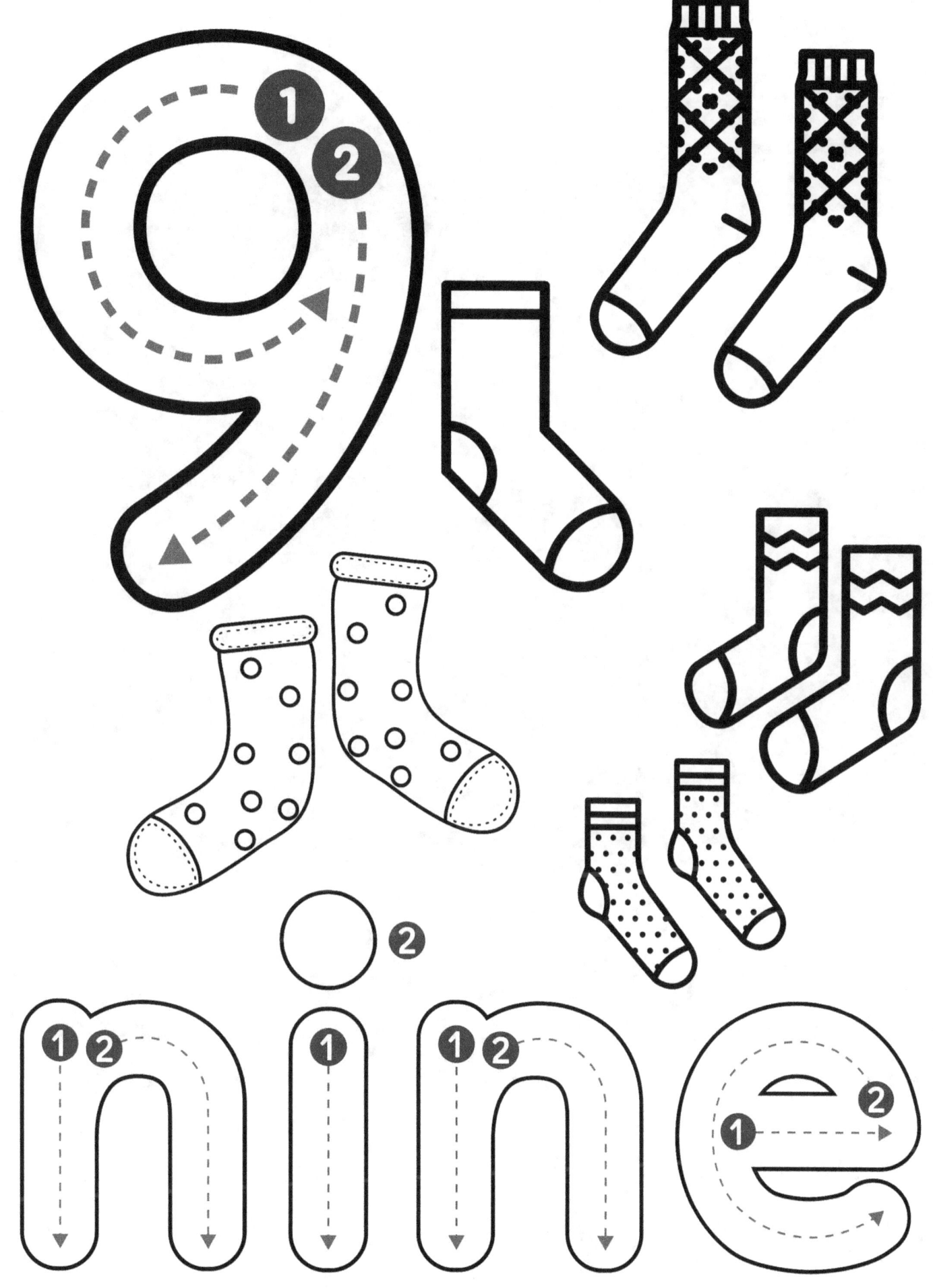

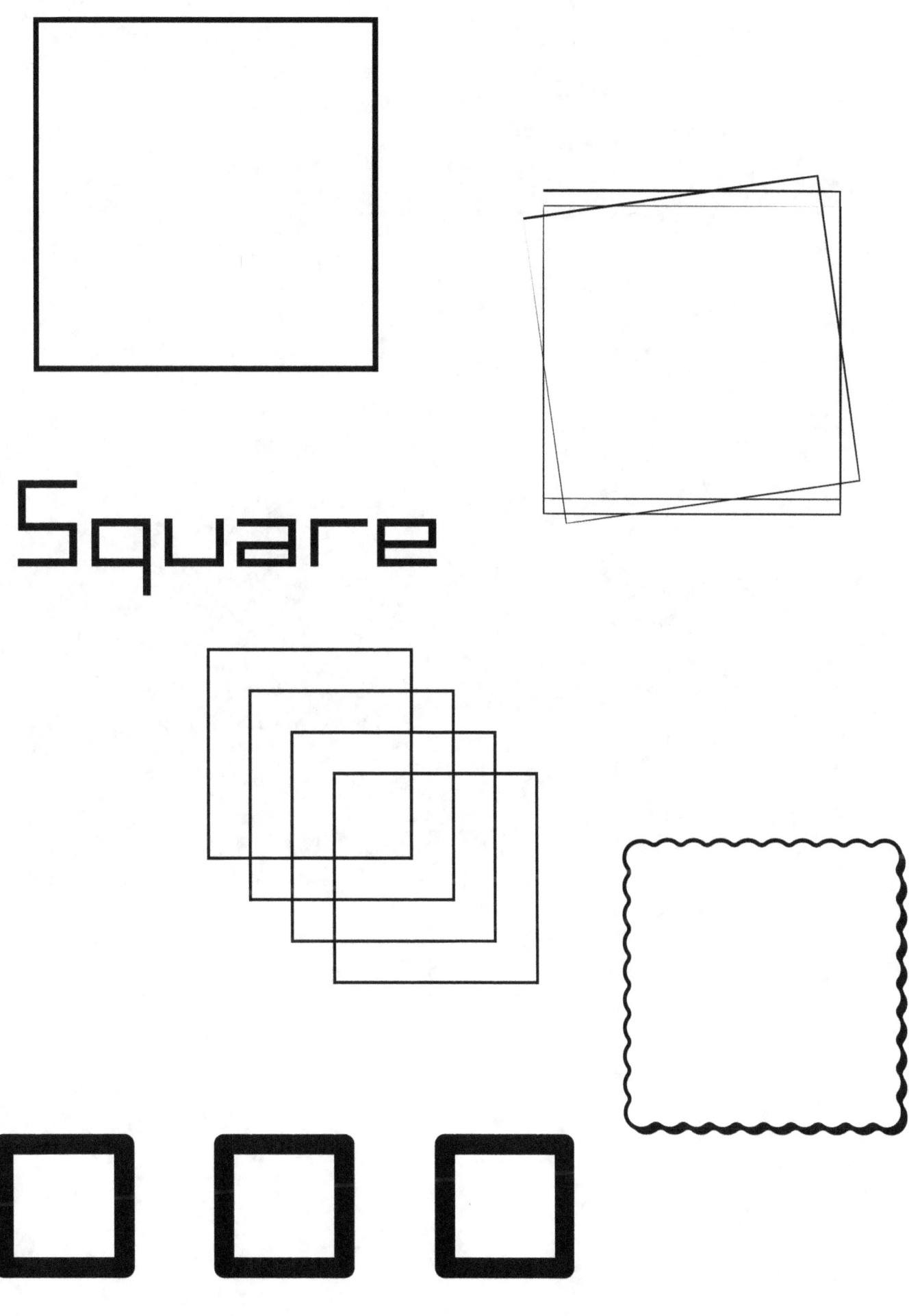

Square

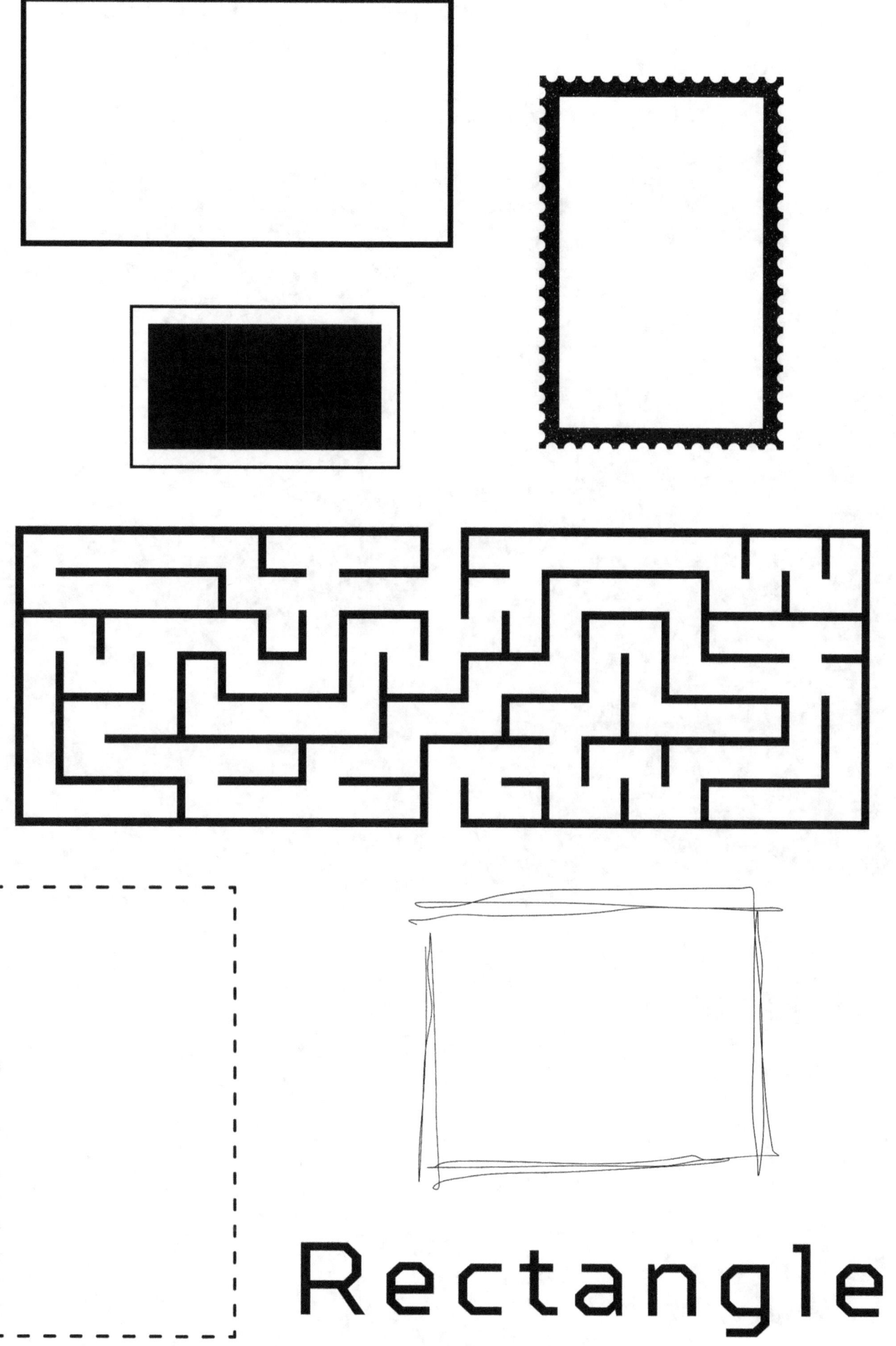

Rectangle

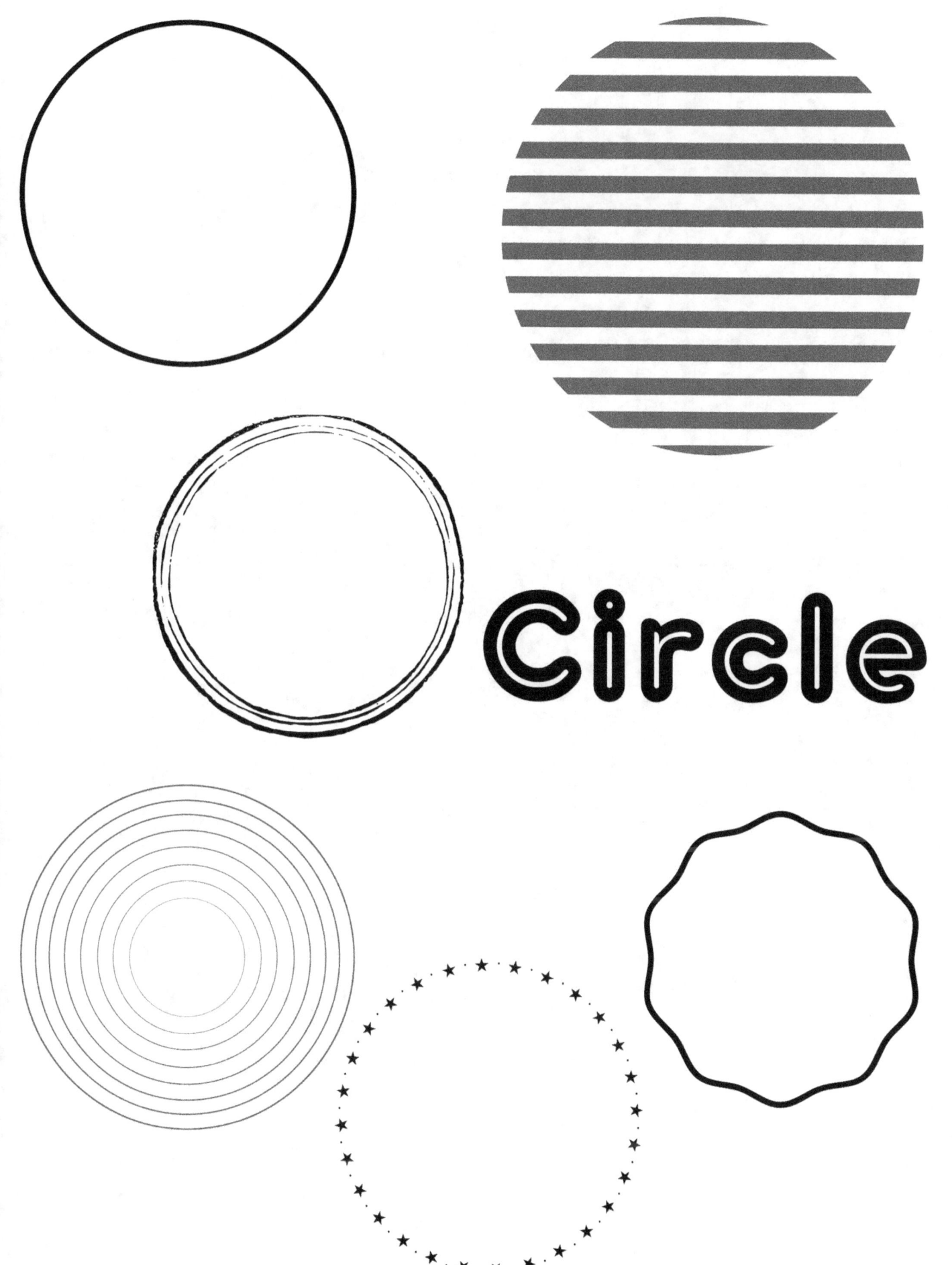

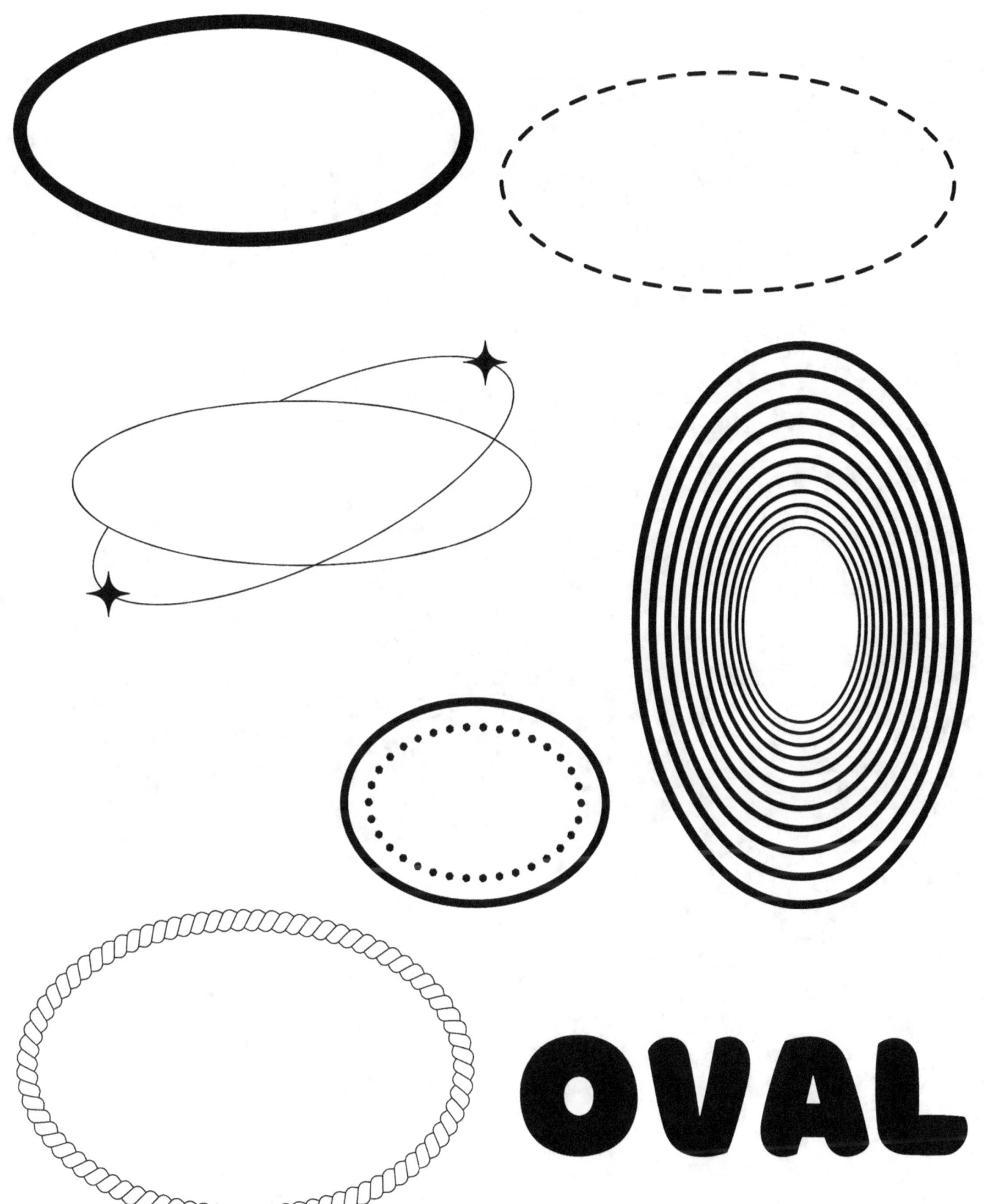

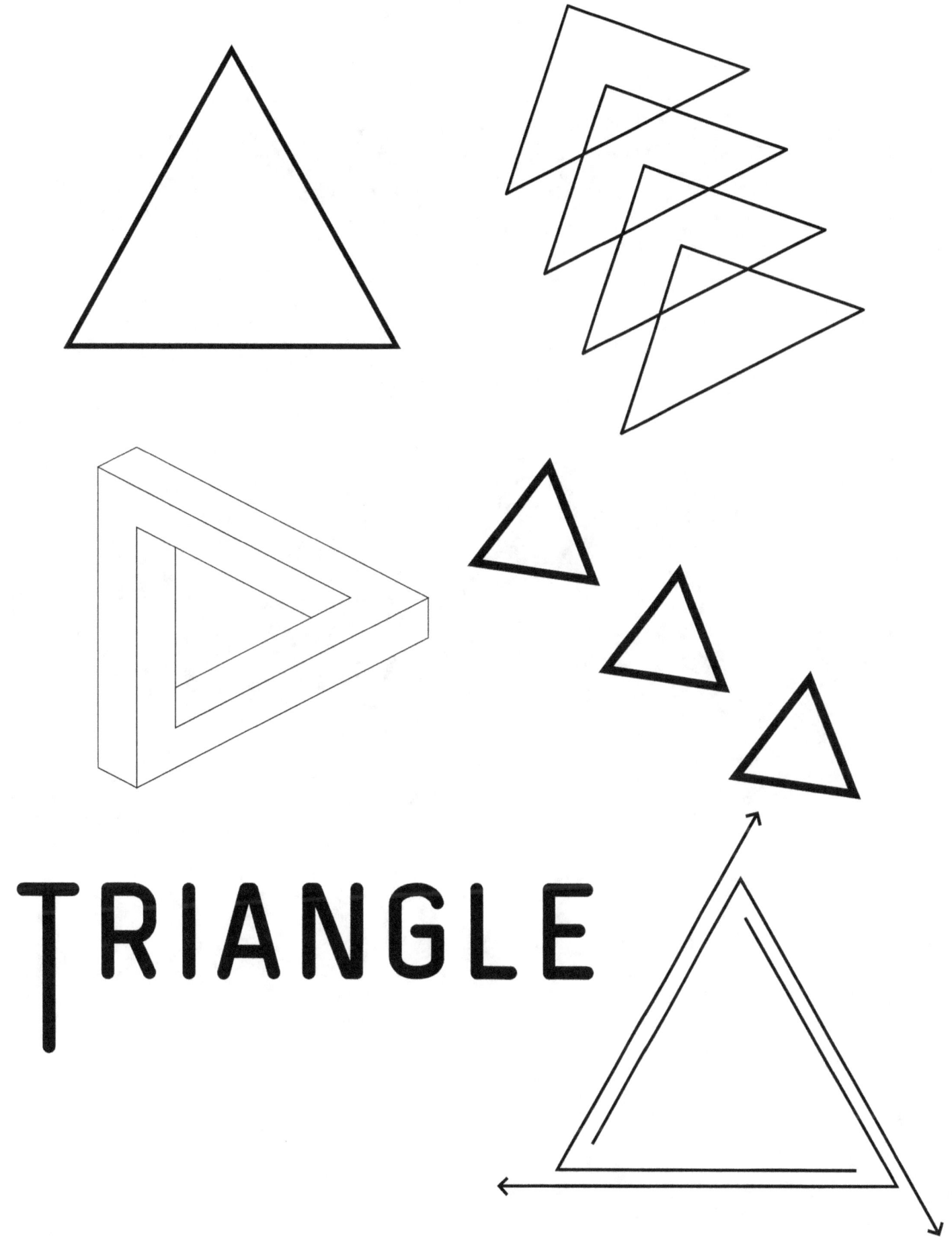

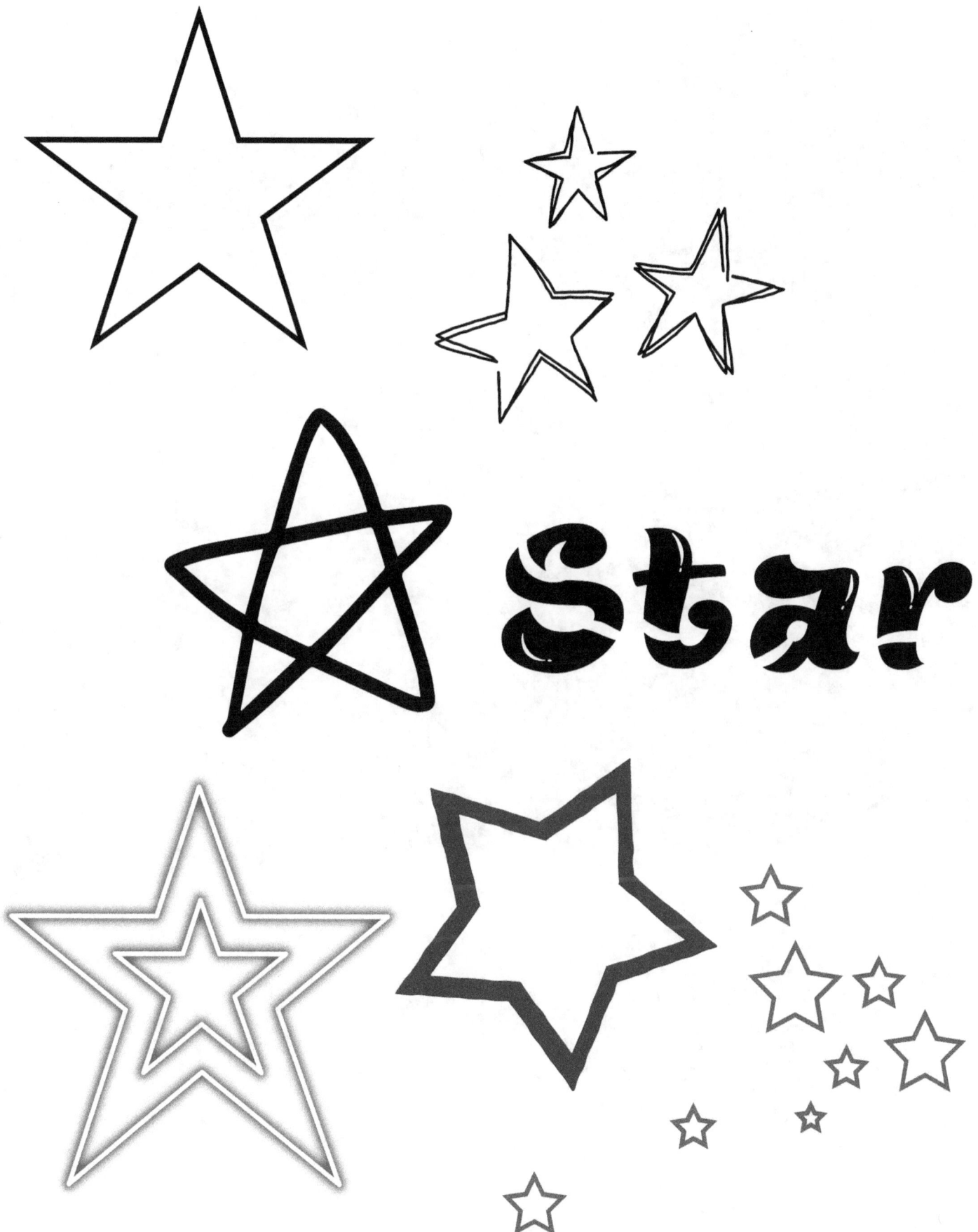

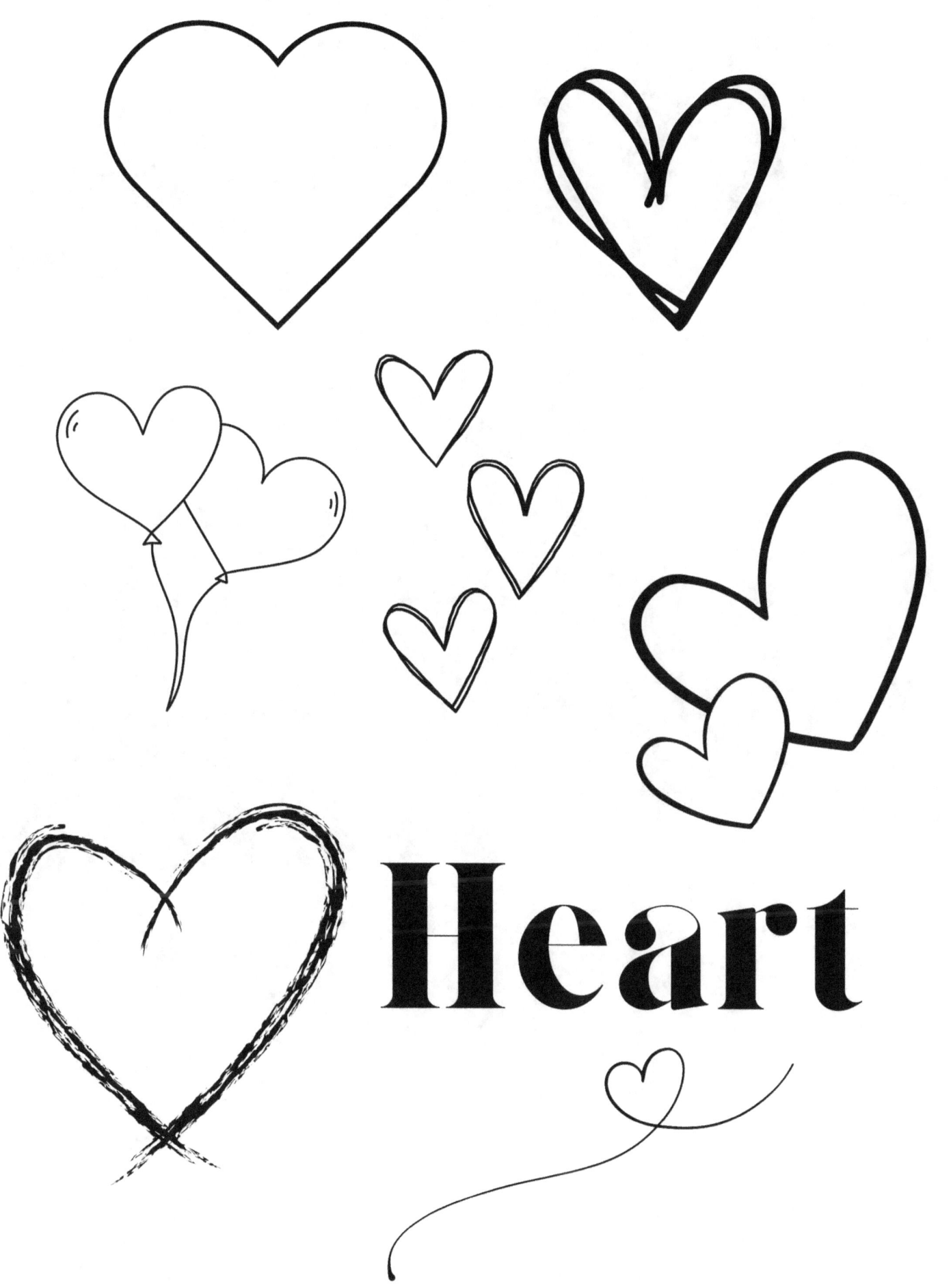

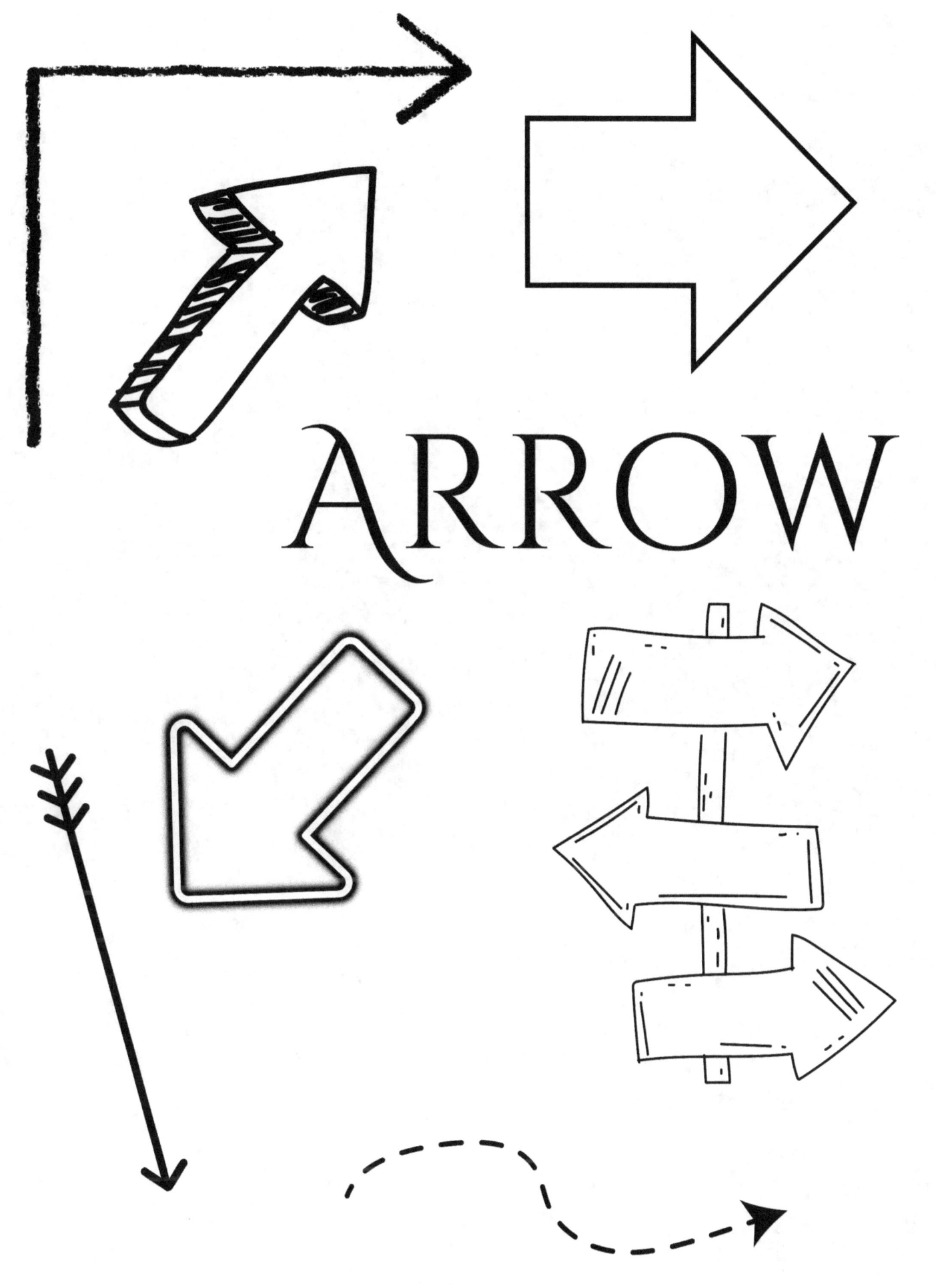

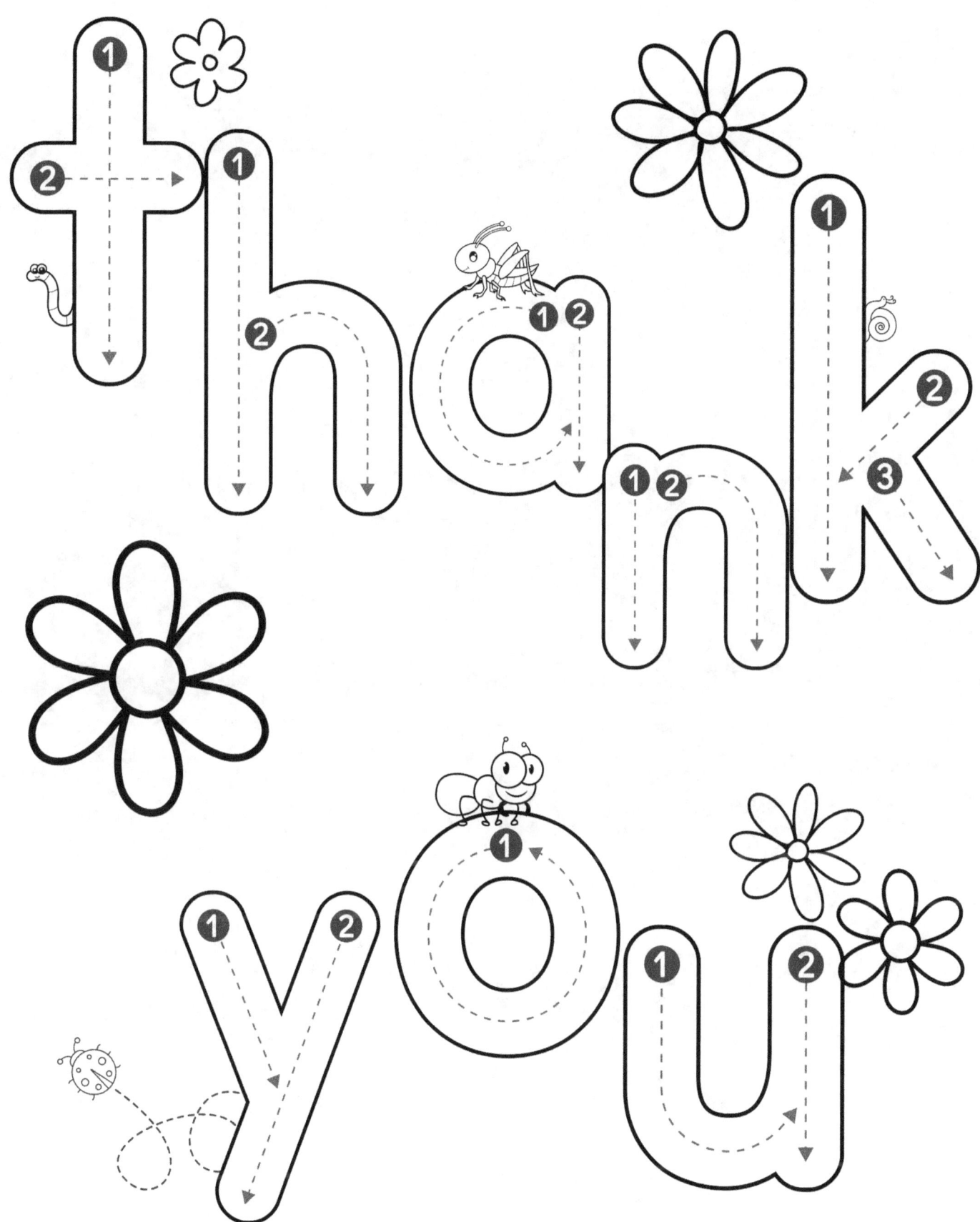

www.ingramcontent.com/pod-product-compliance
Lightning Source LLC
Chambersburg PA
CBHW080514220526
45465CB00006B/2485